ENTERING THE WORKING WORLD

EUROPEAN SCIENCE FOUNDATION

The European Science Foundation is an association of its 49 member research councils and academies in 18 countries. The ESF brings European scientists together to work on topics of common concern, to co-ordinate the use of expensive facilities, and to discover and define new endeavours that will benefit from a co-operative approach.

The scientific work sponsored by ESF includes basic research in the natural sciences, the medical and biosciences, the humanities and the social sciences.

The ESF links scholarship and research supported by its members and adds value by co-operation across national frontiers. Through its function as a co-ordinator, and also by holding workshops and conferences and by enabling researchers to visit and study in laboratories throughout Europe, the ESF works for the advancement of European science.

Further information on ESF activities can be obtained from:

European Science Foundation
1 Quai Lezay Marnésia
67000 Strasbourg
France

Entering the Working World

Following the Descendants of Europe's Immigrant Labour Force

Edited by

CZARINA WILPERT
Technical University, Berlin

Gower

Aldershot · Brookfield USA · Hong Kong · Singapore · Sydney

Published by
Gower Publishing Company Limited
Gower House
Croft Road
Aldershot
Hants GU11 3HR
England

Gower Publishing Company
Old Post Road
Brookfield
Vermont 05036
USA

British Library Cataloguing in Publication Data
Entering the working world : following
   the descendants of Europe's immigrant
   labour force. — (Studies in European
   migration).
   1. Minorities — Employment — Europe
   I. Wilpert, Czarina II. Series
   331.6'094   HD8378.5.A2

Library of Congress Cataloging-in-Publication Data
Entering the working world.
   Bibliography: p.
   Includes index.
   1. Alien labor—Europe. I. Wilpert, Czarina.
HD8378.5.A3E58   1988   331.6'2'4   87-30058

ISBN 0-566-05645-3

Typeset in Great Britain by
Guildford Graphics Limited, Petworth, West Sussex.
Printed in Great Britain by
Biddles Limited, Guildford and King's Lynn.

Contents

Preface

The international and interdisciplinary study 'International Migration and the Cultural Sense of Belongingness of the Second Generation' was launched at the initiative of the European Science Foundation (ESF) in 1980. The objectives of the projects affiliated with the ESF initiative were to study the evolution of the immigrant worker communities and the ethnic identity options of the offspring of the immigrant workers in eight European countries: Austria, Belgium, France, the Federal Republic of Germany, the Netherlands, Sweden, Switzerland and the United Kingdom. At least two different immigrant nationalities were studied in each country. One of the products of the study is the present series of three volumes which address complementary aspects about the future of the new ethnic minorities in a changing European context. This study has been under the leadership of an international and interdisciplinary board of scholars since its inception, among these were Michel Oriol (France), Henri Tajfel (the United Kingdom), and Czarina Wilpert (the Federal Republic of Germany). In addition Julian Pitt-Rivers, Emil Temime and Michael Posner have acted in an advisory capacity.

The first book of the series, *Immigrant Associations in Europe*, studies the social organization and institution building of certain immigrant nationalities in France, the Federal Republic of Germany, the Netherlands, Sweden, Switzerland, and the United Kingdom. This is the first publication on a European level to analyse the internal organization of the immigrant communities and to discuss the ideological alternatives they offer to the following generations. One of the interesting features of this work is that the studies show that immigrant associations are not a transitional phenomenon, but that they gain renewed strength as they come to fulfill changing functions as communities become more established and settled. (Editors: John Rex, University of Warwick, Daniele Joly, University of Warwick and Czarina Wilpert, Technical University of Berlin.)

The second book in the series, *Entering the Working World; Following the descendants of Europe's immigrant labour force*, examines the labour market experiences of the offspring of the immigrant workers, while taking into consideration the different contexts of the labour market framework, economic and policy conditions in each of the European countries in question. At the same time it includes original findings on the training, occupational status, work and mobility orientations of this new generation in comparison to their indigenous peers and the generation of their parents. This book focuses on immigrant and ethnic minority youth in Belgium (Moroccan and Turkish), the Federal Republic of Germany (Turkish and Yugoslav), Great Britian (Asian and West Indian), and Switzerland (Italian and Spanish youth). (Editor: Czarina Wilpert, Technical University, Berlin.)

The third book in the series, *New Identities in Europe; Immigrant ancestery and the ethnic identity of youth*, presents findings from studies of identification patterns and identity structures of the descendants of immigrants: Finns, Turks and Yugoslavs in Sweden, Muslim Pakistanis and Greek Cypriots in Britain, and Spaniards in the Netherlands. The authors are social psychologists and sociologists. One common point of reference in their studies is the conceptual framework of Identity structure analysis which also offers instruments for empirical research. (Editor: Karmela Liebkind, Helsinki University.)

1   From One Generation to Another: Occupational Position and Social Reproduction – Immigrant and Ethnic Minorities in Europe

Czarina Wilpert

Introduction

The studies in European migration undertaken at the initiative of the European Science Foundation (ESF) set out to investigate the issues surrounding the question of the 'cultural sense of belonging-ness of the second generation' – the descendants of Europe's migrant workers. The concept of the cultural sense of belongingness referred to the shared values and aspirations expressed in the daily lives, affiliations and choices of the offspring of first-generation foreign workers. The first book published in this series, *Immigrant Associations in Europe* (Rex *et al.* 1987), provided the framework for understanding the cultural context within which the generation now entering adulthood reach maturity. Case studies about certain immigrant communities in formation, such as the Pakistanis and Greek Cypriots in the United Kingdom, the Portuguese and Italians in France, or the Turks in Germany, inform the reader about the emerging institutions, values and ideologies.

This book reports on findings from studies in five labour-importing countries (Belgium, France, the Federal Republic of Germany, the UK and Switzerland). Some seven million descendants of foreign workers are estimated to live in Europe's post-war recruitment countries (Widgren 1986). The majority of these young people live in the above five countries.

The focus

The work a person does is one of the central determinants of his or her social position. Since the first generation of foreign workers came to work only temporarily, filling certain labour market needs in the receiving society, the authors of the following chapters concentrate primarily on an analysis of the current and future occupational position and work-related behaviours and values of the descendants of immigrants.

In Europe today, initial observations about the situation of the 'second generation' have concluded that the children of foreign workers do inherit the positions of their parents upon entering the labour market (Widgren 1986). They also noted that, in the countries of 'immigration' foreign and minority youth face situations that tend to 'favour a certain reproduction' of the foreign and minority work force from generation to generation (OECD 1981; Castles 1984). This question is also at the centre of our interest. It is not, however, easy to pursue.

As the British, French and German chapters which follow clearly illustrate widespread transformations in the structure of the economy and labour-market participation are in process. Youth in general, and foreign and minority youth in particular, belong to segments of the population most affected by these changes. In order to appreciate variations in these trends among the labour-force-recruiting countries, some important background factors with respect to historical context, 'guest' worker and immigration policies will be reviewed, as well as the employment and unemployment trends amongst youth and other sub-groups of the labour force. Before delving into these questions, some terminological difficulties need explaining, as these repeatedly arise when addressing the immigrant question in Europe.

Immigrants or ethnic minorities?
A plethora of terminological and related conceptual difficulties confront the student of international migration in Europe today. These deserve at least a brief clarification, starting with the usual terms of immigrant, emigration and immigration countries. Some European countries do not recognize immigration; in others, the 'immigrants' are already citizens. The difficulty extends to the question of whether it is possible to speak of second-generation migrants. In the classic countries of immigration in the 'new world', the children of immigrants were known as the second generation. This meant that it was their parents, the first generation, who immigrated; the second generation was, strictly speaking, born in the new country. However, even where there were grey areas, for example children born abroad but who immigrated with their parents, they too were thought of as the second generation. In Europe, this term has become wrought with political controversy. There are a number of reasons for this, for example in the UK, the ancestors of today's ethnic minorities migrated from abroad. They arrived as members of the Commonwealth, and were consequently British citizens (*see* pp. 56–88). Another reason for dis-

satisfaction with the term second generation is because it is thought to stigmatize these young people even further, labelling them as outsiders from one generation to the next. The signifiance of the term second generation in immigration countries has to do with the nationality laws common to these countries, where nationality according to *jus soli* may be obtained by birth. This is not common practice in most European countries. In France, however, young people born in the country become French citizens at full legal maturity, unless they refuse. The Federal Republic of Germany does not recognize itself as a country of immigration, and thus there are neither first- nor second-generation immigrants, but strictly speaking either migrants or foreigners.

In this book, the term descendants of immigrants has been preferred. These are the children of migrant, foreign or immigrant workers who may or may not have been born in their parents' country of origin; they may or may not be citizens of their current country of residence. As will become evident, each country has its own vocabulary specific to the legal, historical and political circumstances of the international migration phenomenon. In the UK, the descendants of immigrants are black and Asian ethnic minorities; in France, they are young foreigners or French of foreign origin. In Belgium, the Federal Republic of Germany and Switzerland, they are the offspring of migrant workers, young foreigners, or, at times in Switzerland, the descendants of immigrants. In every case they are identified as a class apart, marked by their parents' migration history. Only in the cases of the UK, where they are citizens, and in France, when they are born in the country, is it possible to speak of a right to citizenship. Moreover, both the UK and France have a complex recent history of colonialism, which, at a specific point in time, aligned rights to citizenship with their then political interests as the dominating colonial powers. France is, however, the only one of the above countries that has had an outright policy of immigration and assimilation, for economic, demographic and military reasons (*see* pp. 89–110). For this reason, it will be necessary to outline briefly some of the major historical and policy distinctions between the countries in question, which have resulted from their recent histories and immigration policies.

The European framework: legal and institutional factors
Three major factors distinguish the legal status of migrants and their descendants in the countries under study. These are: (a) whether or not there has been a history of colonialism and how its decline fuses with the need for migrant labour; (b) a country's labour recruitment policies and regulations; and (c) its nationality laws, including its self-definition as an immigration country. Colonialism and the

logic of Commonwealth nationality laws have particularly determined the situation of the descendants of migrant labour, the majority of whom in the UK entered as New Commonwealth citizens. In France, colonialism has played a different role: one of its largest contingents of foreign-worker nationalities are the Algerians, who, for the most part, opted for Algerian citizenship at independence.

France is further set apart in being the only European country with a history as a country of immigration before the contemporary European labour migration began in the 1950s. Characteristic of this is the nationality law in France, which, at age of legal maturity, gives the right of citizenship to all children born in the country of foreign parents, unless refused by the individual. This basic right to citizenship for the children of immigrants can be expected to have a major influence on the long-term planning, civic participation and the perceived legitimacy of life in the country of 'immigration'. Unfortunately the right of citizenship is not sufficient in itself to solve other inequalities of discrimination, denigration and sub-stratification of populations of immigrant descent. However it does provide the legitimate basis for political participation.

The third element conditioning the status of the descendants of immigrants is the comprehensiveness of its foreign-worker policy. This is best known as the 'guest' worker system, so named originally in the 1950s in post-war Germany. The term in itself is a euphenism for a system that authorizes entrance into the country strictly with respect to specific labour market needs on a temporary basis, and which ties a worker's residential permit to the terms of his or her work permit. The immigration context of Switzerland and the Federal Republic of Germany exemplify this system, which has functioned in another form in Belgium, and to a lesser extent, also in France. This system institutionalized the legitimacy of the ideology of return. A worker recruitment system existed only sporadically and in a limited way in France and the UK, since their colonial policies and nationality laws permitted a more 'laissez faire' policy of labour migration.

Within this context through a series of international bilateral treaties there exists a stratification of legal rights amongst foreign worker nationalities. This is possible because of the influence of membership in supra-national bodies. In the case of the European Community this membership provides an additional element which moderates the extensiveness of the application of 'guest' worker conditions to migrants. This, for example, has been the case for member countries of the European Economic Community (EEC). Originally, citizens of full-member countries of the EEC had the right of free movement within member countries. Taking another example, Switzerland, which is not a member of the EEC, has been able to control migration flows from Italy, and thereby also its unemployment rate. A similar argument might be used in Germany and Belgium where Turks and Morrocans do not have the protection of EEC membership, which certainly added to the attraction of these workers for official recruitment policy in the last phase of labour recruitment.

The legal and institutional factors that differentiate the conditions faced by the descendants of immigrants upon entering legal maturity and the labour market fall into the following categories: (a) the right to citizenship; (b) the right to join parents working and residing in the European receiving country; (c) the right to bring marriage partners from abroad; and (d) the right to a work permit. (For greater detail on these conditions *see* the appendix, p. 20).

In addition to all this, the descendants of post-war foreign and immigrant workers are now at somewhat different points in the development of the labour-migration cycle in the various receiving countries. In their own way, each of these chapters also reflects not only the maturity of the immigration factor in the respective receiving society, but also the maturity and extent of reflection that has gone into this question from a variety of angles and disciplines. Maturity, in this context, refers more to the length of time and specific historical experiences with the fact of immigration, and not necessarily a qualitatively better status of the immigrants and their descendants.

Who has moved where? The magnitude and origins of immigrant populations

Between 1975 and 1982 the proportion of foreigners to natives in most of the five countries in question has been fairly constant, between 7 to 9 per cent, except for Switzerland where its foreign population has averaged about 15 per cent (Werner and König 1984). The data on France stems from its last census (in 1982). The significance of the size of the population of foreign origins in France is much greater than first apparent and more so than in the other countries, since a considerable share of the descendants of immigrants accept French citizenship at maturity. In the strict sense of the term, however, Germany continues to have the largest foreign population resident within its borders, although these foreigners contributed to little more than 7 per cent of the total population in 1985 (*see* Table 1.1). The size of the foreign population tells little, however, about the annual migration flows. As illustrated in the case of Germany until 1985, they have been major. Table 1.1 gives an idea of the number of foreigners in four of the five countries discussed

Table 1.1 Size of foreign population in selected countries, between 1976 and 1985, thousands

Year ending	Belgium	France	Germany	Switzerland
1976	851.6	–	3948.3	958.6
1977	869.7	–	3948.3	932.7
1978	876.6	–	3981.1	898.1
1979	890.0	–	4143.8	883.8
1980	903.7	–	4453.3	892.8
1981	885.7	–	4629.8	909.9
1982	891.2	3680.1	4666.9	925.8
1983	890.9	–	4534.9	925.6
1984	897.6	–	4363.7*	932.4
1985	846.4	–	4378.9	939.7

*To 30 September.
Source: OECD, *SOPEMI* (1986).

in this book. The UK must be treated separately, since, as Malcolm Cross emphasizes, the ethnic minorities in the UK are in fact the descendants of British colonial citizens (*see* pp. 56–88). As British citizens, they are only partially identifiable as people who have been born in one of the New Commonwealth countries, or children from households where one of the parents has been born there (*see* Table 3.1).

Who are the immigrants? Which nationalities have been most involved in international migration? Apart from the UK whose colonial patterns extended far beyond the Mediterranean, the four most important nationalities involved in international migration across Europe all border on the Mediterranean periphery. The two largest contingents are the Turks and the Italians, each with over 1.5 million migrants throughout Europe. The Turks are predominantly settled, and have a population of over one million in the Federal Republic of Germany. There are also more Italians living in Germany, where they are the third largest nationality after the Yugoslavs, than in any other European countries. The Italians also have very large settlements averaging about 300,000 persons in Switzerland, Belgium and France. In fact, in France, the Italians are probably the largest population of citizens of foreign origins, where they have been immigrating since at least the turn of the twentieth century. Portugal and Algeria have each over 800,000

	Belgium 1983	France 1982	Germany 1985	Switzerland 1985
Austria	–	–	172.5	29.2
Finland	–	–	9.9	1.4
Greece	21.1	–	280.6	8.7
Italy	270.5	333.7	531.4	392.5
Portugal	10.4	764.9	77.0	30.8
Spain	56.0	321.4	152.8	108.4
Turkey	70.0	123.5	1401.9	50.9
Yugoslavia	5.6	64.4	591.0	69.5
Algeria	10.8	795.9	5.3	1.9
Morrocco	119.1	431.1	48.1	1.4
Tunisia	6.8	189.4	23.1	2.1
Other countries	320.6	655.8	1085.3	242.9
Total	890.9	3680.1	4378.9	939.7
As per cent of total population	9.0	6.8	7.2	14.6

Source: OECD, *SOPEMI* (1986).

emigrants throughout Europe, although they are predominantly in France where they are the two largest groups of foreign origins. This is, of course, not fully reflected in the official statistics, which as Palidda and Muñoz explain (pp. 90) do not take into account those who have become naturalized. Algerians, Morrocans and Tunisians taken together, France has a population of about one and a half million immigrants from North Africa. As emigrants throughout Europe the contingent of Yugoslavs abroad is very close in size to that of the Portuguese and Algerians. They are the second largest nationality in Germany and altogether tens of thousands of Yugoslavs are living in Switzerland, Belgium and Austria., (*see* Table 1.2.)

What is the demographic impact of immigrant populations on the age structure within the former recruitment countries? Some idea of this can be gained by studying the relative share of the foreign populations within the total population according to age groups. Table 1.3 gives an idea of the size of the foreign population under 20 years of age in four of the countries concerned. Although the most recent data on the age composition according to nationality

Table 1.3   *Share of young foreigners among all young people between 0 and 19 years, per cent*

	Germany	Belgium	France	Switzerland
	9.1	13.0	7.9	15.7

		Share of total foreign population to total population		
	7.6	8.9	6.8	14.5

Share of young foreigners according to age group

Years	1980		1981		1982		1983	
	Nat.*	For.*	Nat.	For.	Nat.	For.	Nat.	For.
0–9	9.7	15.6	11.9	21.6	12.3	16.9	11.4	13.4
10–14	7.7	8.3	7.0	10.1	7.8	8.9	7.2	7.8
15–19	8.6	8.0	7.9	9.2	8.1	7.5	8.1	8.1

*Nat. = nationals; For. = foreigners.
Source: Le Bon (1986), 23–4.

on a comparative basis is from the early 1980s, its value is that it gives an idea of the relative importance of the factor foreign/immigrant youth in the respective categories compared to the adult foreign population and to their indigeneous peers. Moreover, except for Germany where out-migration continued to be an important factor until 1985, it can generally be assumed that these age cohorts have remained more or less stable. Thus, relative size and ratio of young foreigners in the 15- to 19-year-old category in 1982 can be projected to have entered, with approximately the same proportions, the 20- to 24-year-old category in 1987. This cursory review of the legal and institutional context, the size, origins and demographic composition of the nationalities involved in European migration sets the framework for the comparability of the studies that follow.

International migration, work and cultural belongingness
Immigration situations provide a particularly rich illustration of societal processes. While they may be considered to be specific applications of general laws of social theory, more important may be the insights to be gleaned about social processes in general, inter-group relations and forms of social stratification. Moreover, through their greater visibility, contrasts and comparability with indigeneous

8

groups may permit the observer to learn more about social and cultural change.

What does work and occupational status have to do with the cultural belongingness of the offspring of immigrants? Theoretical assumptions about the processes of adaptation of immigrants underlie this question, and these assumptions should be testable with the emergence of a second generation. On the one hand, their place in the economy demonstrates the extent and nature of their involvement in mainstream society, determining their societal integration and their social mobility. On the other hand, the negative developments of immobility, social deviancy and ethnic substratification of certain immigrant nationalities over generations is thought to be best explained by their cultural values. Even today it is often believed that it is cultural belongingness that hinders social mobility. In fact, cultural versus structural juxtapositioning is best illustrated in theorizing about immigration, acculturation and assimilation.

The penduluum of interpretational frameworks in sociological theories has swung between a search for cultural to structural causes for social isolation, ethnic ghettoization or social maladaptation among some immigrant groups or to explain the successful integration and social mobility among others (Steinberg 1981). Although today's theoretical premises are often much more complex, including numerous variables and elaborate construction of models, in the end they tend to favour one pole or another. It is hoped to avoid this tendency towards reductionism, whilst leaving room for a consideration of cultural factors as an aid towards understanding subjective perceptions and strategies. This means that the relationship between occupational position and migration in Europe must be investigated, and inquiries made into the impact of international migration on the stratification of the receiving societies.

The issues in question

Occupational position is a key to class membership, and the extent of upward occupational mobility from one generation to the next is an indicator of the extent of closure or the permeability of classes. Immigration theories also have to do with stratification, and traditionally the successful integration of immigrant settlers has been measured on the extent of their occupational mobility over the generations. Such a study of the stratification of immigrant minorities in European society presents numerous problems. For example, immigrants are not easily classified. Although it has generally been accepted that the European 'guest' workers initially form an underclass (Hoffmann-Nowotny 1973) – an ethnic or immigrant substratification within the receiving society – this may not always be

9

that pervasive. Leaving their legal status aside, and looking strictly at occupational position, in the German case a subsection (about one-fifth) were recruited for jobs in the primary labour market where there was a shortage of skilled labour (see pp. 122–7).

The first two chapters of this book present two highly contrasting situations in this regard. In the first country, Switzerland, the occupational mobility of second-generation immigrants are studied with respect to their fathers and to the indigeneous working class. At first glance, the findings of this study would seem to refute all notions of occupational inheritance. In the second country, the UK, ethnic minority youth, although recognized as citizens, are about 50 per cent more likely to be unemployed than other popular categories. For this reason alone, the situation of the descendants of migrants from West Indian and Asian origins could be characterized as poorer, both in respect of the previous generation and of indigeneous young white people of the same age group. Superficially, it may appear preferable for people to be immigrants in Switzerland rather than citizens in the UK. When compared with the countries studied, Switzerland presents the best objective occupational and employment conditions for the young adult descendants of migrants. One reason for this could be found in the generally healthier overall economic prosperity in Switzerland. Fibbi and de Rham, however, propose another: the strict Swiss immigration policy, which makes foreign workers a major lever for state intervention in the labour market. The Swiss case is the clearest example of 'guest'-worker control and manipulation for labour-market needs.

Distinct differences in policy are of course not strictly legal issues but rest on a variety of social and economic foundations. These may be related to larger political issues and centre-periphery relations or transformations in the structure of the economy. Some of these changes in the labour market and their signifiance for youth in general and foreign youth in particular will now be discussed.

Labour market trends: youth in Europe in the 1980s
It does not make sense to study foreign or minority youth outside of the larger context of youth in society today. The first wave of descendants of Europe's immigrant workers have reached working age at a period characterized by two antagonistic trends: the coming of age of the European baby boomers and the simultaneous declining participation of youth in the economy. In recent years attention has been directed at the high levels of youth and minority unemployment in all European countries. Youth unemployment must be viewed within the context of the longer range trends in employment and structural changes in the economy. Specialists on youth-employment

Table 1.4 Changes in school and labour market participation of youth (15–19 years) in three European countries, between 1960 and 1970, per cent

	Males		Females	
	School	Labour market	School	Labour market
Belgium	20.5	−17.0	26.6	−7.4
France	17.8	−33.4	19.9	−24.4
United Kingdom	25.2	−18.7	29.4	−15.3

Source: OECD demographic trends 1950–1990. *La Scolarisation* 1960–1980, OECD, Paris, 1978, in Hartmann (1986).

patterns foresee a lengthier period ahead of unstable employment for young people, including unemployment, part-time work, and participation in the informal sector of the economy (Baethge *et al* 1983; Hartmann 1986; OECD 1982).

Since the Second World War, two major phases in the participation of youth in the labour force are observable. The first, until about 1970, witnessed the increase of compulsory schooling and even larger numbers of the youth population staying longer at school. As Hartmann (1986) insists, during this period extended schooling was expected to correlate with better occupational opportunities and more secure employment (*see* Table 1.4). This, too, was the time when foreign labour was recruited and immigrant labour-force participation was at its highest in the economics of Europe.

The second major phase began in the early 1970s, when youth unemployment emerged as a social issue. Along with it, this second phase was characterized by the slow realization that length of education no longer transferred into equivalent occupational security. Youth spoke of themselves as the 'no-future' generation. For youth relegated to the lower streams of compulsory education, schools came to be considered as places where time had to be passed, 'parking lots' before entering out into the real world (Baethge *et al.* 1983). Nevertheless, the quality of education, streams and types of schools attended continued to operate as a selective mechanism, separating the advantaged from the disadvantaged. This situation was particularly glaring in some countries because of the corresponding demographic trends. In some places, the creation of governmental emergency programmes to supplement education and supply pre-vocational training (*see* chapters 3 and 5) was able to delay the process for the population immediately leaving school. In Germany, where this was the case, more and more young people who had completed vocational training in the 20- to 24-year-old age group became subject to unemployment or underemployment. There, in 1985, about 17 per cent of the unemployed were found in this age group (Schober 1986). Moreover, only about half of those who received a qualified occupational training were able to find a job in their field after completion (*see* p. 128).

These and similar observations in other European countries have led to the conclusion that the total amount of work needed in society today is decreasing (*see* pp. 90–111; Hartmann 1986). Other authorities warn that a mismatch exists between aspirations for future occupations and the needs of the economy. A more accurate appraisal might point to the mismatch between occupational-training opportunities and occupational needs.

Foreign youth, like their indigeneous counterparts, are now reaching working age at a period marked by the unpredictability of the future of work and occupations. The structural changes occurring in the European economies suggests the dissolution of traditional and permanent occupational structures. Nevertheless, although there are certain common patterns in the overall trends mentioned above, there exist as well a number of discrepancies and contradictions, which indicate that there are important differences in Europe as well.

Thus, while it is true that youth unemployment is high in a number of European countries, the significance of this factor may differ greatly from country to country. This is connected with rather dramatic differences in the traditional rate of employment in these countries, and the very unequal share that certain sub-groups of the population have played in the labour force. The labour-force participation rates of youth, women and elder workers of both sexes have been of differing sizes, depending greatly on the country in question.

The relationship between changes in rates of labour-force participation, youth unemployment and the status of foreigners

The occupational position of the descendants of immigrants and foreigners in Europe must be seen in relation to the overall status of employment and changes occurring in the past decade or more. Looking solely at the individual case studies of the status of foreign and minority youth in the individual countries is not enough to help the reader grasp the significance of this factor and larger processes that are taking place. If unemployment as a percentage of total labour force between 1960 and 1980 is examined, a gradual

Table 1.5   *Unemployment rates in selected European countries, between 1960 and 1980, per cent*

	1960–69	1970–73	1974–76	1977–79	1980
Belgium	2.2	2.0	4.0	6.7	7.5
France	1.7	2.0	3.8	5.3	6.3
Germany	0.8	0.8	3.4	3.7	3.3
Switzerland	0.0	0.0	0.3	0.4	0.2
United Kingdom	1.7	2.6	3.5	5.4	6.3

Source: OECD (1982), 129.

growth in unemployment in all European countries concerned will be observed. It will also be seen that it is lowest for the two countries most dependent on foreign labour with the tightest regulations covering legal status. In the more highly controlled Switzerland, unemployment is practically negligible, and, in Germany, it is only about half the rate of its neighbours, France and Belgium. By 1985, Germany's unemployment rate had more than doubled (8.3 per cent of the total labour force), but was still 3 to 4 per cent lower than the next highest, Belgium and the UK.

If youth (defined as people under 25 years of age) is specifically examined, very different shares of youth on the overall unemployment rates will be observed in these same countries. (Table 1.6) Already in the early 1960s, youth unemployment accounted for almost one-quarter of the unemployment in the UK, but only 12 per cent in Germany (1968). By 1980, the share of under 25 year olds in total unemployment had more than doubled in Germany, grown by about 15 per cent in the UK, and by a similar rate in Belgium, but to a smaller overall total. In France, where youth have traditionally had a relatively high share of the total unemployment, it had increased only marginally. However, when the relative unemployment in this age category according to sex is examined in Table 1.6, it will be seen that, as a whole, women have suffered a larger share of unemployment in this age group, and that the discrepancy between the sexes has been highest in Belgium, France and Germany, in that order. It has been relatively equally distributed according to sex in the UK. Switzerland is not shown in Table 1.6, because youth unemployment there is almost negligible.

Three factors emerge as significant for the relatively low unemployment figures in Switzerland and Germany: a high rate

Table 1.6
Table 1.6 *Youth (under 25 years) as a percentage of total unemployment in selected European countries by sex, between 1960 and 1980*

		Belgium	France	Germany	United Kingdom
				(1963)	(1962)
	male			4.4	13.3
	female			7.8	10.2
	both sexes			12.1	23.5
		(1972)			
1970	male	7.4	20.3	5.4	18.5
	female	9.8	20.6	13.4	7.5
	both sexes	17.2	40.8	18.8	25.7
1973	male	n.a.	18.1	8.3	20.7
	female	n.a.	22.5	15.0	11.5
	both sexes	n.a.	40.6	23.3	32.2
					(1977)
1976	male	10.5	14.6	12.1	20.5
	female	21.8	26.6	16.6	10.3
	both sexes	32.3	41.2	28.7	40.8
1979	male	9.2	14.7	9.2	19.0
	female	21.8	25.6	16.9	21.6
	both sexes	30.9	40.3	26.1	40.6
1980	male	8.9	13.4	10.8	20.4
	female	20.5	30.4	16.5	15.3
	both sexes	29.4	43.8	27.3	38.3

Source: OECD (1982), 134–41.

of foreign labour recruitment, coupled with marginal legal status through the 'guest'-worker system and the ideology of return. This enabled Germany, for example, to reduce the absolute number of people economically active in manufacturing and construction in the decade between the early 1970s and 1980s at the expense of foreigners, who accounted for about 45 per cent of the redundancies between 1974 and 1977 and over half between 1980 and 1982 (Table 5.4). This is well illustrated by a study of the in- and outflows of foreigners in Germany during this period. Between 1974 and 1977, there was not only a negative balance of over (−)433,264 outflows, but the outflows were primarily among former workers,

	1975	1979	1983	change
United Kingdom	71.4	71.0	64.4	−7.0
Germany	65.2	64.6	59.4	−6.8
France	64.5	64.0	60.6	−4.5
Belgium	61.2	59.6	56.5	−4.5

Source: Therborn (1986), 70.

who totalled over 457,000 people. Thereafter, in the next period between 1982 and 1984 over 373,487 more foreigners left Germany than entered. The majority of those who left between 1983 and 1984 belonged to the economically active population.

An additional significant factor for understanding the divergent trends in youth and foreign-youth unemployment is connected with the role of another major ascending segment of the labour force in several economies – women. In order to appreciate the status of sub-groups in the labour force, it is instructive to look at the rate of employment of the total adult population (15 to 64 year olds) between 1975 and 1983 in the countries concerned. In Table 1.7 it will be seen that the employment rate of the entire population was higher in the four relevant countries in 1975 than less than a decade later. Also, contrary to popular interpretations, the reduction in the share of workforce employed in this period is almost as great in Germany, with its relatively low unemployment figures as it is in the United Kingdom, with higher overall unemployment rates. This is another indication that the 'guest' worker system has masked the real extent of unemployment in Germany, where it was possible to reduce its labour force at the expense of foreign workers, a policy not available in the UK where colonial immigrants are citizens with a legitimate right and expectations to remain in the country. Moreover, the employment rate for the adult population was still higher in the UK in 1983 than in Germany.

Once more, from the employment participation rate according to sex, it can be seen that, despite reductions in overall employment and youth unemployment, there has been a general trend in a number of European countries towards increased labour-force participation of women between 1975 and 1983. In 1975, there were already different rates of participation, the lowest in Belgium (43.9 per cent) and the highest in the UK (55.3 per cent). Germany and Switzerland

Table 1.8   *Rates of female participation in labour force in 1975 and 1983, per cent*

	1975	1983	change
Belgium	43.9	49.4	+5.5
United Kingdom	55.3	57.5	+2.2
Germany	49.6	49.6	+0.0
Austria	47.9	50.3	+2.4
Switzerland	49.6	48.6	−1.0
France	49.9	52.1	+2.2
Finland	65.6	73.5	+7.9
Sweden	67.6	76.6	+9.0

Source: Therborn (1986), 71.

are the only two of the five countries under discussion where women's participation in the economy did not increase between 1975 and 1983. In fact, there was a 1 per cent decrease in women's participation in Switzerland (Table 1.8). As Therborn's (1986) recent study succinctly argues it is not much easier to explain rates of employment than it is unemployment rates. Nonetheless, it is very likely that the changes in employment rate for different sub-groups of the population are not only indicators of a segmented labour market, changes in the occupational structure and the nature of jobs within certain countries, but also new potentials for mobilizing certain sectors of the population to enter the labour market. At this stage it is not possible to explain youth unemployment by the ascendancy of women.

Not apparent from the above discussion is the change in labour-force participation for other sub-groups, for example teenagers (15 to 19 year olds). According to the 1982 OECD study, the most dramatic decline in labour-force participation took place among teenagers. By the 1960s, this had already set in in Germany and had reached its low in the 1980s, the years when the first descendants of foreign workers began to enter the labour market. A similar pattern can be seen in France. Only in the UK, where 67 per cent of this age group either work or are unemployed, has the decline been less dramatic. The difference is, however, that in Germany these youth had become involved in education or training programmes, which kept them out of unemployment figures until they are over 20 years old.

The same study shows that the category of the labour force with the traditionally highest participation rate in three of the countries under consideration (France, Germany and the UK) has been in the 20- to 24-year-old males. Since the early 1960s, there has been a gradual decline in all three countries in their participation rate, accompanied by a steady increase among women in this age group. These trends reflect widespread changes in the composition of the labour force, but the actual extent of reductions in jobs may not be as great between countries as was first thought. The impact it has may, however, vary greatly for different segments of the population – youth, foreign youth and women. The studies that follow must be seen in this context.

Some common issues and main themes in the European studies

Despite legal historical distinctions between countries where labour recruitment originated in the 'guest'-worker form (Germany and Switzerland), and the less controlled private recruitment and attraction of workers from overseas colonies (France and the UK), the differences between immigration and non-immigration countries, distinct alien and nationality laws and finally a variety of heterogeneous movements within the labour market, certain structural similarities can be found across countries. Some studies underline certain of these common tendencies more than others. Migration cycles (*see* pp. 150–74) and streams (*see* pp. 89–110) occur in each of the countries, and each of these cycles has not only received a different reception, more or less favourable, but also they were often composed of distinct nationalities and sub-groups. The last to enter have frequently had the least opportunities. All countries cast their foreign and ethnic minorities into social hierarchies of preference, which often are a manifestation of legal and institutional status, but may also carry a racist potential.

Economic restructuring has hit the labour markets of all countries studied. The following cases treat primarily its effects on the descendants of immigrants. Where its effects appear to have been less dramatic, there is an apparent tie to the coupling of foreign-worker and labour-market policies (that is, in Switzerland and Germany).

All of the following chapters address the issue of the occupational position of the descendants of immigrants and the related question of the extent of social reproduction of an immigrant strata within the labour market. These issues are tackled very differently. Each chapter singles out certain themes, which it treats in greater depth. The order of presentation also reflects the weight placed on certain issues and the breadth of the perspective, moving from somewhat larger empirical studies of the native and foreign youth, including the analysis of macro-social and political issues, to the more subjective micro-social studies of the responses and strategies of the generations in question.

Only in Switzerland was it possible to study indicators of inter-generational mobility in comparison with the native population. The French, German and British studies have used a combination of secondary-data analysis and original data on sub-groups to achieve this comparison. As might be expected, official policy towards foreigners plays a greater role in the Swiss and German cases than in the others. In Switzerland, immigration policy is viewed as an instrument of labour-market manipulation. In the UK, the question of political implications must be posed differently. Neither immigration nor labour-market policy are of prime concern, since the first is more or less historically settled, and the second evidently practically non-existent. The interpretive framework rests on a study of labour-market training schemes and their differential utility for ethnic minorities and the white majority. Behind this, Cross sees a political postulate, which turns the cause and effects around, explaining declines in employment as evidence of lower levels of employability. For a substantial share of minority youth in the UK, it is less a question of social reproduction and more one of downward mobility. Because of widespread unemployment and the precarious-ness of jobs, many are worse off than the previous generation. Observations in France, Germany and Belgium coincide with these findings.

France, according Palidda and Muñoz, has aspects of legal structural conditions that combine elements of the British (colonialism, racism and citizenship) with the tighter controls of the Swiss and German 'guest'-worker systems. The authors argue that the typical trajectories and opportunities of young people of foreign origin correspond with their legal status. However, racism and colonialism intervene to assign the visible descendants of north African workers, French or not, to the lowest social status.

None of the authors finds a strict social reproduction of the 'immigrant'-worker underclass. All findings suggest a more complex pattern of stratification and a variety of response strategies. The segmentation of economies for different classes and sub-groups of workers emerges throughout Europe, but the descendants of foreigners, by and large, continue to occupy the lowest rung of the social hierarchy. This is visible even in Switzerland, although there are tendencies for the foreigners to be better qualified there than the parent generation. The common theme in the UK, Germany, France and Belgium is partial reproduction. A rather significant share of these young people are worse off than their parents, slipping into the marginal reserve, which Bastenier and Dassetto classify as the 'sub-proletariat'.

In the studies that address youth's subjective aspirations, perceptions and strategies *vis-à-vis* entry into the world of work or their visions of their occupational futures, questions are raised about social reproduction via family socialization. Bastenier and Dassetto go so far as to ask whether young people from immigrant backgrounds are properly socialized for life as workers. This approach assumes that during socialization children develop expectations, competences, values and life goals, strategies for dealing with their environment and a sense of their place in society. This includes an understanding of the given and perceived opportunities and constraints. For many of the descendants of migrant workers in Europe it is not clear within which society they have a rightful place. Moreover, migration goals were to better the status of the whole family. The initial orientation on the home country and the experience of success, relative to their original situation and reference groups in the country of origin, influence the goals and socialization environment within the family. Generalizations are difficult without taking into consideration the social history of the family and the reference groups of both generations. Here a number of problems arise.

Occupational status in the 'country of work' may not reflect the status held before migration. He/she may stem from other social classes in the country of origin, whether it be the peasant rural classes, skilled tradesmen, the 'petite' bourgeoisie, the lower echelons of the civil service, or the higher ranks of industrial labour. This social status, moreover, may have little to do with the immigrant's self-perception of social position and membership group. First-generation 'immigrants' live in two societies, and often see themselves primarily with reference to the society left behind. These distinctions are not only difficult to evaluate with respect to the future opportunities of the first generation in the immigration context, but they may be significant for the kinds of goals a person sets for his or her children and the resources he or she is able to muster for their future. First-generation migrant families may also be differentiated according to background factors and the social resources they have at their disposal. (This approach has been useful to achieve an understanding of the variability to be found in the situation and strategies employed by members of the Turkish second generation in Germany.) There are social resources that may defy or support theories of social reproduction.

Studies of inter-generational mobility are best made at a

comparable point in the life-cycle of two generations. Life-cycles are, however, not strictly biological, but are socially defined. Is the social definition of the proper point in the life-cycle to begin work, to become independent or to marry and have a family determined by the context of the 'immigration country' or by the traditional values of the family and the culture of origin? In the countries of advanced industrialization, youth has been prolonged, whereas in some of the countries of origin, the parent generation married, founded a family and went out to work before the age of 20. How comparable is the same biological age of two generations in two different socio-historical settings?

Class membership and subjective identification with work, culture and nationality figure in the following studies, conducted among Spanish and Italian youth in Switzerland, Morroccan and Turkish young people in Belgium and Turks in Germany. In the Swiss case, the authors observe a 'bilaterality of references' (Catani) amongst the descendants which they relate to a generational continuity in language and cultural references as well as a permanent anchorage (without citizenship) into the everyday reality of the new community. In the German case, the role of the settlement process for affiliation, identification and work-values has been studied. Here, too, even within one nationality – Turks in Germany – it is not possible to conclude that there exists a homogeneous second-generation community. In this context, references to cultural belongingness and identification with the culture of origin are used to interpret strategies young people develop when they and their parents have not been able to fulfil the goals of the migration enterprise, rather than as an explanation of their current social status. Although the evidence does not point to complete social reproduction, in certain countries substratification and sub-proletarian tendencies for many descendants are apparent, and in all cases there are signs of ethnic stratification of the immigration country. Nevertheless, in France, Germany and Switzerland a minority of young immigrants have been able to use resources to take steps towards achieving a better future. It remains to be seen whether ethnic stratification will lead to widespread ethnic mobilization, for which the 'Beurs' movement among young foreigners of north African origins in France (see p. 104) may be a first indication.

Appendix

Legal distinctions characteristic of the five receiving countries
The descendants of immigrants have the right to citizenship: in France at 18 years of age if they were born in the country. In

the United Kingdom, if they are born in the United Kingdom, or born from parents or grandparents who were born in the United Kingdom, or if they are the children of immigrants who have become citizens. A right to citizenship does not exist for the children of foreign workers in Germany or Switzerland. In Germany a foreigner may apply for citizenship after eight years of residence; in Switzerland 12 years residence is required. In both countries they may become citizens as dependent children if their parents apply and are accepted for citizenship. So far not more than one per cent of the foreign worker nationalities have obtained citizenship in either country. (Note: the right to citizenship exists in the Federal Republic of Germany solely for *Auslandsdeutsche*, people who are considered to have German nationality because their parents or grandparents were born as German citizens into the German Reich. These people contribute to the greater majority of persons becoming German citizens each year. The nationality laws have recently been changed in Belgium to make it easier for the children of immigrants to become citizens (OECD 1987).

The right to join the family resident in the European receiving country In Germany, children under 16 years of age have the right to join their parents. If children have remained or been sent to the country of origin for schooling they must return before 16 years of age, with the exception of the state of Hessen and the city-state of Bremen, where the age is 18 years.

In Switzerland the children of foreigners had, until 1986, the right to join their parents until the age of 20 years. In 1986 this age limit was reduced to 18 years of age for all foreign worker nationalities except Italians.

In Belgium children aged 18 or younger (until 1984, it was up to the age of 22) may join their parents working in the country. Since 1984, this right must be applied for within one year following the parent's migration (Taverne 1985).

In France, in general, children may join their parents up to 18 years of age. An exception is made, however, for the daughters of Spanish and Portuguese residents, who are allowed entry until they have reached the age of 21.

In the UK children up to 19 years of age may generally join their resident parents, and dependent, single daughters may join until they reach 21 years of age. This, however, applies only to a minority, since the dependent children of citizens also have British citizenship and the right to enter and depart the country as other citizens.

Marriage partners of the children of immigrants In Germany, eight years' uninterrupted residence and full legal maturity (18 years) is required, and, moreover, the marriage must exist for at least one year (in Bavaria, three years) before legal residence of the spouse is permitted. In the UK the spouse of a woman resident in the country may join only if she is herself a British citizen, and it is proven to be a real marriage (Groth 1985). In Switzerland the foreign spouse of a foreign resident may, theoretically, at least, join their partner abroad at any time.

Work permit restrictions These exist for foreign youth joining parents resident in Belgium, France and Germany, not for those in the UK and Switzerland. In France since 1984 the issue of work permits are dependent on three uninterrupted years of residence in the country. These regulations are slightly less significant and less complex than they were in the early 1980s.In Germany, however, the children of foreign workers, who do not have either a permanent residence permit (*unbegrenzte Aufenthaltserlaubnis* or *Aufenthaltsberechtigung*) or at least five consecutive years of residence, do not have the same right to work as do Germans, EC migrants and foreigners with permanent resident permits. According to a representative study (König *et al* 1986) this was the case for about 55% of the 15 to 24 year old Turks, the single largest nationality, in 1985.

References

Baethge, M. (1983), 'The significance of work for young people under the current situation in the Federal Republic of Germany', in P. Grootings, *Youth and Work in Europe Vol. II., Comparative Research and Policy Problems*, Moscow: Academy of Science (USSR), 29–40.

Baethge, M., Schomburg, H. and Voskamp, U. (1983) *Jugend und Krise – Krise aktueller Jugendforschung.*, Frankfurt: Campus.

Campani, G., Catani, C. and Palidda, S. (1987) 'Italian immigrant associations in France', in Rex et al, *Immigrant Associations in Europe*, Aldershot: Gower.

Castles, S., Booth, H. and Wallace, T. O. (1984) *Here for Good, Western Europe's New Ethnic Minorities*, London: Pluto Press.

Castles, S. and Kosack, G. (1985), *Immigrant Workers and Class Structure in Western Europe*, London: Oxford University Press.

Groth, A. (1985), 'Bürgerliche und politische Rechte der Wanderarbeitnehmer in der E.G.' in Just, W. D. and Groth, A. (eds), *Wanderarbeiter in der E.G.*, Mainz: Matthias Grunewald Verlag, 32–40.

Hartmann, J. (1986), *To Live on the Brink: Causes and Consequences of the Decrease in Youth Employment in Europe*, an unpublished report on the research project Integration of Youth into Society, Uppsala.

Hoffmann-Nowotny, H. J. (1973) *Soziologie des Fremdarbeiterproblems*, Stuttgart: Enke Verlag

Just, W. D. and Groth, A. (eds.) (1985), *Wanderarbeiter in der EG*, two volumes, Mainz: Matthias Grunewald Verlag.

König, P., Schultze, G., Wessel, R. (1986), *Situation der ausländischen Arbeitnehmer und ihrer Familienangehörigen in der Bundesrepublik Deutschland*, Represäntativuntersuchung 1985, Bundesminister für Arbeit und Sozialordung: Bonn.

Kühl, J. (1987), 'Zur Bedeutung der Ausländerbeschäftigung für die Bundesrepublik Deutschland', in Helga Reimann and Horst Reimann (eds), *Gastarbeiter*, Opladen: Westdeutscher Verlag.

Lebon, A. (1986), 'Les jeunes issus de l'immigration: effets de leur présence sur la situation demographique de quelques pays d'emploi;, *Studi Emigrazione*, **81**, 21–34.

Maillat, D. (1987), 'European receiving countries in the OECD', in OECD, *The Future of Migration*, Paris: OECD.

OECD (1981), *Young Foreigners and the World of Work*, Working Party on Migration, Paris: OECD.

OECD (1981–1987), SOPEMI, *Continuous Reporting System on Migration*, Paris: OECD.

OECD (1982), *The Challenge of Unemployment*, Report to the Labour Minister, Paris: OECD.

OECD (1983), *Migrants' Children and Employment: The European Experience*, Paris: OECD.

OECD (1985), *Employment Outlook 1985*, Paris: OECD, 47–63.

OECD (1987a) *Immigrants' Children at School*, Paris: OECD.

OECD (1987b) *The Future of Migration*, Paris: OECD.

OECD (1987c), *The OECD Observer*, **145**, April/May, Paris: OECD.

Piore, M. J. (1979), *Birds of Passage: Migrant Labor and Industrial Societies*, Cambridge: University Press.

Rex, J., Joly, D. and Wilpert, C. (1987), *Immigrant Associations in Europe*, Aldershot: Gower.

Schober, K. (1986), 'Aktuelle Trends und Strukturen auf dem Teilarbeitsmarkt für Jugendliche', in *Mitteilungen aus der Arbeitsmarkt-und Berufsforschung*, **3**, 365–370.

Steinberg, S. (1981), *The Ethnic Myth: Race, Ethnicity and Class in America*, Boston: Beacon Press, 13.

Taverne, M. (1985), 'Belgien', in Just, W. D., Groth, A., *Wanderarbeiter in der E. G.*, Mainz: Matthias Grunewald Verlag.

Therborn, G. (1986), *Why Some Peoples Are More Unemployed than Others: The Strange Paradox of Growth and Unemployment*, London: Verso.

Werner, H. and König, I. (1984), *Ausländerbeschäftigung und Ausländerpolitik in einigen Westeuropäischen Industriestaäten*, Nürnberg: Institut für Arbeitsmarkt-und Berufsforschung, Reihe Beitra 89.

Widgren, J. (1986), 'The position of "second generation" migrants in Western Europe: policy failures and policy prospects', *Studi Emigrazione*, **81**, 7–20.

Wilpert, B. (1983), 'Youth and work in the Federal Republic of Germany — recent research evidence', in P. Grootings, *Youth and Work in Europe*, **I**, National Reports, Moscow: Academy of Science (USSR), 23–122.

23

2 Switzerland: the Position of Second-Generation Immigrants on the Labour Market

Rosita Fibbi and Gérard de Rham

Immigration context and labour market

Immigration to Switzerland: the background

Having emerged from the Second World War with an unscathed industrial infrastructure, Switzerland relied chiefly on imported labour to turn the wheels of her industry. As early as 1960, foreign residents in the country numbered roughly 500,000. By 1970, their ranks had swollen to nearly a million (938,000), 60 per cent of whom were employed. A further 229,000 held jobs but had no residence permit (seasonal workers and frontier commuters).

In the 1970s, prompted by a sharp backlash of xenophobia, the Swiss authorities endeavoured to reduce the number of foreigners – efforts that were greatly abetted by a timely economic recession. By 1980, foreigners residing in Switzerland totalled 893,000, of whom 56 per cent were gainfully employed. Some 77 per cent of residents held a permanent-residence permit, usually granted after ten years in the country, placing them on an equal footing with nationals for employment; these permit holders then accounted for 52 per cent of foreign workers. Meanwhile one-third of all foreigners held a residence permit that was renewable on an annual basis and likely to be accompanied by an authorization to work. This latter category (18 per cent of foreign manpower) was 'monitored': its access to the labour market and geographical and occupational mobility remained under the jurisdiction of the authorities responsible for employment policies. The legal system made the hiring of this category of workers particularly flexible, especially in the 1960s, when it constituted the largest group (72 per cent in 1960). Seasonal-worker status has been institutionalized in Switzerland. Holders of this type of permit work up to nine months of the year at 'seasonal activities', mainly in the construction and hotel sectors, and must leave the country for the remainder of the year. Their families are not allowed to join them. Finally, there is a fourth type of authorization to work: the 'frontier-commuter' permit. Holders must return to their own country at the end of each working day.

The hiring of these last two categories of workers is constantly monitored by the authorities. The portion of foreign labour they represent has varied widely from one year to the next, ranging from 42 per cent in 1973 and 31 per cent in 1981 down to 28 per cent in 1984 (*La Vie Économique*, November 1984). In August 1984, frontier commuters numbered 207,000. In the same year, monitored labour as a whole totalled 11 per cent of the country's wage-earners. Given the fact that they are not considered residents, seasonal workers and frontier commuters are not taken into account when the ratio of foreigners to the overall population is calculated. (This latter ratio stood at roughly 15 per cent at the last census, in 1980.) Nor do they produce a second generation, given that their offspring stand a very slim chance of being allowed to reside in Switzerland.

Among residents, the largest ethnic groups are Italians (47 per cent), Spaniards (11 per cent), Germans (10 per cent), French (15 per cent), Yugoslavs (5 per cent) and Turks (4 per cent). Traditionally, the socio-occupational status of the north European immigrants has tended to be higher than that of newcomers from southern countries. Foreigners account for 16 per cent of the overall population in the 0 to 15 age bracket, 15 per cent from 16 to 19 years, 8 per cent from 60 to 64 years and 5 per cent for those 65 and older (*La Vie Économique*, April 1986).

Lastly, it should be noted that there is no legal mechanism – as in France for example – whereby young foreigners are automatically naturalized. On the contrary: the process, which may only be initiated after 12 years' residence in the country, is long, probing and, in most cantons, costly. As a result, very few foreigners acquire Swiss nationality: the proportion has steadied at roughly 1 per cent of the foreign population, following a peak of 1.5 per cent in 1977, largely owing to the coming into force of new birthright legislation allowing women to transmit Swiss nationality to their offspring under certain conditions. In 1985, minors under 16 years of age accounted for 20 per cent of naturalized citizens, corresponding roughly to their proportion in the immigrant population.

This chapter will deal more exclusively with the socio-occupational integration of young foreigners. A comparison will be drawn with Swiss youth of the same age group, based on national statistics supplemented by the findings of recent studies. With this in mind, it seems appropriate to glance at the patterns of the labour market and its behaviour, together with training and hiring policies practised by the authorities.

Labour market policy in Switzerland

Set within a very free-enterprise oriented social system, and being at odds with state intervention in economic life, the labour-market policy in Switzerland is defined as a set of measures aimed at ensuring equilibrium between the supply of, and demand for, labour on a short-, medium- and long-term basis. The policy strives, in particular, to enhance the circumstances enabling those categories in difficulty to secure gainful employment (OFIAMT 1980: 28–31). The aims of the policy are functional (economic) capacity of the labour market, full employment and a guarantee of sufficient income for the unemployed, together with personal and social safeguards for the working population.

The major instruments of this policy are occupational training, control over foreign workers, unemployment insurance and labour legislation. While labour legislation has not evolved much over the past two decades (albeit with the advent of mandatory accident insurance), other sectors have been the scene of fundamental political debates resulting more often than not in revised legislation.

Immigration policy (officially referred to as 'alien manpower policy') was one of the most controversial issues in Swiss politics throughout the 1960s and 1970s. Although opponents of a 'foreign invasion' were unsuccessful in enforcing their party programmes designed drastically to reduce the immigrant population, their impact played a major role in the quotas placed on the number of foreign workers. Equally unsuccessful was the bid by a number of unions and parties defending workers to abolish the discriminatory status of seasonal worker. Even the very limited revision of the alien law, passed by Parliament, was rejected by a plebiscite. Screened by this legislative deadlock, governmental and administrative practices consolidated. Out of the various permits emerged two categories of immigrant workers: a 'secure' majority allowed to be occupationally mobile and entitled to bring in their families; and those allowed in on a temporary basis – without their families – to hold specific jobs (seasonal workers and frontier commuters, along with those granted annual permits during their qualifying period and a limited number granted permits of short duration). A large contingent of foreigners also work illegally in Switzerland and, as a result, do not figure in official statistics, as well as slipping through the social security net. The institutionalization of the distinction drawn between secure workers, be they Swiss nationals or non-Swiss granted long-term residence, and other foreign workers of temporary or revocable status, has many repercussions.

While a well-defined trend in economic studies tends to view overall supply and demand on the labour market as uniform aggregates, it is clear they actually differ markedly. The demand for labour, for example, is not distributed evenly for different skill standards. Bottlenecks sometimes occur at the very top of the occupational ladder. This is revealed by analyzing the educational standards of immigrants: foreigners are over-represented among holders of a university degree (7.2 per cent as opposed to 5.3 per cent Swiss, according to the federal census in 1980) (OFS 1985). Hutmacher (1981) emphasizes the special importance of this imbalance in a labour market heavily weighted by the tertiary sector (roughly 75 per cent) such as Geneva's. Despite this, until recently the most frequent situation – statistically speaking – saw a need for semi- and even unskilled labour, which, in fact led to heavy immigration. The census revealed that immigrants having little education vastly outnumbered their Swiss counterparts (36 per cent, as opposed to 19 per cent of the nationals). Among other factors, the very common process of social mobility in the past 30 years has clearly helped increase demand for this skill category (Weiss 1986).

The authors believe that a shifting partition of the labour market, not unlike the one described by Piore (1973) in the United States, is apparent in Switzerland. Piore outlines two employment markets, which differ in their institutional, technological and economic organization. The primary market includes steady, well-paid jobs requiring average to high qualifications, whereas the secondary market comprises insecure, poorly-paid jobs offering no chance for internal promotion. Mobility between the two spheres is relatively limited. The secondary market also acts as a buffer in boom-and-bust situations (Abrahamsen *et al.* 1986: 91). A recent empirical study reveals the 'trend towards a split' in the Swiss labour market, which is blamed of 'relative assimilation of occupational fields', as well as demand-side segementations, for example through the creation of internal labour markets and strict wage hierarchy (*Commission pour les questions conjoncturelles* 1986: 6).

It is felt that these trends are apparent in the way immigrant manpower has been employed over the years. Up until the recession of the mid-70s, the secondary market tended to swallow up all foreign workers, since the majority were controlled by the authorities who granted and renewed their permits and thereby confined them to jobs seldom solicited by nationals. This was proved by the fact that (in 1976) up to 40 per cent of holders of the longest-standing permits left the country when the number of jobs was reduced (*La Vie Économique*, April 1986).

Following these cuts in 1976, the employment policy was again aimed at dividing the 'indigenous working population' – which included both the Swiss and holders of long-standing residence permits – from the rest of the work force, for which no collective term was invented (OFIAMT 1980). By means of subtraction, this category included seasonal workers, frontier commuters, seekers of asylum, illegal immigrants and a number of annual permit holders. The OECD draws this same distinction by dealing separately with permanent residents and foreigners who are not permanently settled (OECD 1985).

A further 'qualitative' measure was implemented, earmarking a number of new authorizations for highly skilled labour: executives, experts, researchers and so on (Hug 1986: 15). When the legislation covering occupational training and unemployment insurance was revamped, the opportunity arose to specify the aims and measures of both sectors. The existing law on occupational training (Loi Fédérale sur la Formation Professionelle) was passed in 1978 and came into force at the beginning of 1980. It was in no way radically novel, as it maintains the predominance of apprenticeships. Apprenticeships run in most cases along dualistic lines: the apprentice is indentured by a firm where he is overseen by a skilled tradesman four days a week, while on the fifth day he studies theory at a vocational school. An apprenticeship, which may last from two to four years depending on the trade, is successfully completed when the candidate is awarded a *Certificat Fédéral de Capacité* (CFC; federal certificate of capacity). Despite strong union opposition, the law also provides for 'elementary training' of short duration. The *Union syndicale* (the main labour league) further advocated extending classes in vocational schools, monitoring those firms training apprentices more closely and including apprentices in collective agreements. The league did not achieve its aims, as the referendum it initiated against the existing law was rejected. The development of elementary training has therefore remained very limited. Cantonal authorities have made this type of training subject to special authorization, granted when a regular apprenticeship is not possible. In 1984, official agreements for elementary training accounted for 2.3 per cent of indentures, with variations ranging from 0 to 5 per cent in the different cantons (*La Vie Économique*, April 1986).

The occupational-training system turns out a special brand of worker, who is bound by an employment contract. The market for apprenticeship positions is therefore part and parcel of the labour market. A portion of trainees attend vocational schools on a full-time basis, schools which award the same diplomas as business and industry. A 'popular initiative' (amendment to the Constitution by plebiscite), launched by far left-wing party, advocated the expansion of these schools to afford everyone access to the vocational training of his choice. The initiative also called for substantial development of continuing education (upgrading and recycling), a field that has not attained a desirable standard, despite a number of new provisions in the 1978 law. This view is even held by the director of the Federal Commission for Industry, Arts, Trades and Labour (OFIAMT), who is responsible for the labour market policy as a whole (Hug 1986: 3). Objections by the major parties and unions led to the rejection of this initiative, as expected.

The unemployment insurance sector, by contrast, has been the scene of genuine innovation. In quick response to the advent of unemployment in 1974 and 1975, a provisional unemployment insurance scheme was established, which became permanent following legislation in 1982. Unemployed people qualifying under the fairly strict requirements of this law are entitled to a substitute income for 250 working days. These benefits amount to 70 or 80 per cent of an insured income, dictated by the number of dependants concerned. However, they are set on a diminishing scale corresponding to the length of unemployment, despite left-wing and union opposition. A number of preventive measures were also implemented, aimed in particular at encouraging the geographical and occupational mobility of workers.

Generally speaking, then, the labour-market policy relies more on stimulation and co-operation with business and industry than on centralized, interventionist measures. Apart from unemployment insurance, which derives to a large extent from social policy, the exception to this principle is the immigration policy (Maillat 1974). Foreign workers, therefore, serve as the major lever for state intervention on the labour market. An opportunity study forecast that this role has been attributed to them for a long time to come (Freiburghaus 1985: 77). This observation is all the more significant in the wake of other opportunity forecasts on labour potential, which show that the declining birth-rate will not reduce the supply of labour substantially before the end of the century, and that an 'unemployment potential' higher than in the past is likely in coming years (ibid.: 10).

Evolution of the labour market
Since the end of the 'Glorious Thirties', Switzerland has endured two periods of heavy recession resulting in fairly sharp downturns in employment. Between 1974 and 1976, some 330,000 jobs were eliminated, representing over 10 per cent of the working population. The 1981–83 recession was less serious, wiping out some 65,000 jobs. The departure of large numbers of immigrant workers explains why the unemployment rate has remained so low (official figures

list roughly 1 per cent of workers as jobless). Those who returned to their native countries numbered some 245,000 in 1974–76 and some 20,000 in the early 80s; they therefore 'absorbed' three-quarters of job eliminations during the first recession and 30 per cent during the second (ibid.: 6 and 5). A number of these departures were due to non-renewal of (annual or seasonal) permits. The rest were 'voluntary' departures of workers entitled to remain in Switzerland. The economic process, together with the portrayal of immigration as a temporary phenomenon, were thus to blame along with the legal provisions of the immigration policy. Unemployment became a Swiss export commodity on a level with capital, watches and chocolate. However, the difference between the two periods of recession demonstrates that this 'solution' to employment problems will no longer prove workable in future.

The majority of workers who considered returning home in case of real or possible job difficulties have departed, and employment prospects in the native countries of those who would consider doing so now have dimmed. The number of fluctuating immigrants can no longer be reduced significantly without jeopardizing certain sectors (especially the construction and hotel-restaurant industries), where they hold strenuous and often poorly-paid jobs that attract few other people seeking employment.

It should be stressed that the exodus of immigrants not only eased the strain on the Swiss labour market, but also caused the exodus of young foreigners along with their parents and a concomitant reduction of the 'second generation'.

The structure of the socio-occupational distribution of foreigners differs from that of Swiss citizens. The 1980 census revealed that 69 per cent of the non-Swiss working population resident in Switzerland was made up of blue-collar workers, as opposed to a mere 35 per cent of working Swiss nationals. White-collar workers (discounting executives) accounted for 21 per cent of foreigners, as opposed to 41 per cent of the Swiss. A mere 7 per cent of immigrants (Swiss 11 per cent) were self-employed. These discrepancies are, however, less pronounced than in the 1970 census, which revealed 78 per cent blue-collar and 17 per cent white-collar workers among gainfully employed foreign residents.

Youth on the labour market

Although Switzerland has been spared the massive youth unemployment problems besetting other European countries, the young account for a large number of the unemployed (40 per cent). Along with women, foreign workers, older workers and the disabled,

Table 2.1 *Percentage of people seeking employment based on age bracket*

Years	Swiss	Non-Swiss	Non-Swiss/Swiss
15–19	0.87	3.33	3.8
20–24	1.91	4.84	2.5
25–29	1.20	1.90	1.6
30–34	0.69	0.80	1.2

Source: OFS (1985).

young people are considered by the OFIAMT as a special group and to be more vulnerable on the labour market (OFIAMT 1980). A recent study drafted under the auspices of the Swiss Science Council singled out people making their debut in the working world as a potential 'problem group'. Since foreigners and unskilled workers were also deemed problem groups, among others, the report epitomized the case of unqualified young foreigners as a collocation of ill-fated attributes capable of producing exceptionally high unemployment rates and especially lengthy periods of individual unemployment (Freiburghaus 1985: 87).

Official unemployment statistics include only those workers who are registered at employment agencies, thereby underestimating the total number. Federal census data is more reliable, as it takes stock of people seeking employment. The result is also clearer. In December 1980, the census revealed that 28,000 people were in search of a job, that is, 0.9 per cent of the working population. This percentage varies according to nationality, and is nearly twice as high among immigrants (1.46 per cent) as it is among Swiss citizens (0.77 per cent). The rate is also much higher for the young than for more mature people.

The greater 'sensitivity' of young jobless foreigners should be pointed out – a plight that is quite familiar in other European countries but almost unknown and even unsuspected by the public at large in Switzerland, including the immigrant community itself. Recent figures attest to the persistence and even the worsening of unemployment among youth. In 1986, young people between 15 and 20 years of age accounted for 4.6 per cent of all those unemployed drawing benefits, while those between 20 and 24 years totalled 18.5 per cent and the 25- to 29-year-old group totalled 16.5 per cent. Thus, about 40 per cent of those completely unemployed were under 30 years old. The number of young women exceeded that of young people as a whole by nearly 30 per cent (OFIAMT data: *La Suisse* 12 June 1986).

Young foreigners: formal education and training

In theory, both the schooling and occupational training of immigrant children must be given by the educational system of the canton of residence. As far as compulsory education is concerned, schools offering the curricula of native countries (mainly Italian and Spanish) may only be attended on a provisional or extra-curricular basis. Generally speaking, young foreigners receive schooling and vocational training which lead to Swiss diplomas.

Despite this, a study conducted in Zurich revealed that, in the not too distant past, either by exception or periodic returns to Italy, over 10 per cent of Italians born in 1963 completed their compulsory education at an Italian school (Gurny *et al.* 1984: 22–23). Access to apprenticeships is rarely possible for this group, which undoubtedly explains the presence of Italian-language vocational schools, most often established by Italian unions and subsidized by the Italian and Swiss governments. A dispute has arisen between these schools and the Swiss and Italian educational authorities over funding and the recognition of diplomas. In French Switzerland, it seems that all compulsory education takes place in Swiss schools (FIPES III 1985), and there are no Italian-language vocational schools.

The issue of mutual recognition of diplomas, especially vocational certificates, has long been debated in bilateral negotiations between Switzerland and immigrants' native countries. This was particularly discussed at meetings of the Italian-Swiss Commission, although no agreement emerged. Switzerland grants no systematic recognition of foreign vocational certificates, and makes recognition subject to equal requirements for the corresponding Swiss diploma – requirements that are seldom met. By contrast, it appears that, for all intents and purposes, Italy recently waived the principle of reciprocity and accepted the validity of diplomas earned in Switzerland, so as not to place Italian nationals returning home at a disadvantage.

Regional idiosyncrasies of the labour market

The economic cycles of the 1970s and 1980s have led to increased inter-regional disparity on the employment front. The large urban centres (Zurich, Basel and Geneva – although it should be recalled that they are 'large' only by Swiss standards in a country totalling only six million inhabitants) witnessed fairly sizable gains in the number of jobs available. At peak activity in the industrial and tertiary sectors during the 1970s, employment surged by 25 per cent in these centres. Nearly 40 per cent of all jobs are now concentrated in these areas.

One type of region saw a significant reduction in the number of jobs available: the peripheral and traditionally industrial Jurassian arc as well as the north-east of Switzerland. Nearly 10 per cent of jobs there have been lost in the last 10 years. The serious decline in the watch-making industry – the near-exclusive livelihood along the Jura mountains – brought particularly dire consequences to the area. Not only is unemployment rapidly rising, but both the resident and working populations are declining, despite a firm tertiary sector and a measure of diversification in the production of machines. For over a century, the arc of Jura was a target for immigration; it has now become an area of depopulation. Small- and medium-sized industrial or tertiary-based centres have maintained their employment levels and still account for over 40 per cent of all jobs. Outlying agricultural and tourist areas have done likewise, at times aided by local industry. Despite this, they account for a mere 10 per cent of all jobs (Brugger 1985: 13–17 and 79–94).

The choice of three regions as the focus of this study was based on these differences, as well as the fact that all three are French-speaking.

The place of young foreigners of the labour market: a comparison with young nationals

The entry of young Swiss and non-Swiss into the working world

Quantitative aspects Every year, approximately 85,000 to 90,000 young people residing in Switzerland complete their compulsory education, of whom 11–12 per cent are foreign nationals. The numbers of cohorts grew extensively in the early 1980s, as larger classes reached adolescence. At the age of 15 to 16 years, young people are faced with one of the major decisions of their lives: occupational integration. Several avenues are open: (a) continuation in school to the junior college level (baccalaureate) or in general education or occupational training; (b) apprenticeship; or (c) to head directly into working life. The proportion of young people who choose between these different alternatives varies considerably from one region to the next. The main reason for the discrepancies is that, since the cantons are jealous of their sovereignty over education, each has its own school systems with its own particular features. The federal government assumes responsibility, however, over junior college programmes (baccalaureate) and

Table 2.2   Educational standard of 16 year olds in 1983, per cent

General education	16.6
Occupational training	41.0
Total post-compulsory training	57.6
Total of all educational standards	85.9

Source: OFS, *Statistiques des élèves* (1983/84).

occupational training, especially where apprenticeships are concerned. (While not disregarding cantonal differences, the issue of integration of young people on a national scale will first be examined).

Most young people who complete their compulsory education undertake an apprenticeship. In the mid-70s, over two-thirds of boys and one-third of girls chose this course. In 1983, the proportion of boys in occupational training (apprenticeship or full-time vocational school) fluctuated round the 70 per cent mark, whereas the number of girls rose over the previous decade to reach 47 per cent (CESDOC 1985: 71)

Between 1976 and 1983, the number of young foreigners beginning occupational training in business, industry or at school doubled, jumping from 6,000 to 12,000. Relatively speaking, the proportion of immigrants in occupational training also grew: from 8.6 per cent in 1976 to 13.1 per cent in 1983, for the first year of occupational training.

Table 2.3 illustrates the importance of the demographic factor more empirically than factually. These figures do not take into account the number of young foreigners returning home, or the number of people not continuing training after compulsory education. Nevertheless, the comparison is legitimate.

The prescribed layout for training programmes sets Grade 9 as the final year of compulsory education and Grade 10 as the first post-compulsory year. Comparing the two, it would appear that the increasing number of foreigners in occupational training is attributable to a larger immigrant pupil population in school until 1980–81. Subsequent to this period, other factors come into play, such as greater availability of state training facilities (officially accessible since 1980 to all young people, regardless of permits), a greater propensity on the part of young foreigners – mainly girls – to invest in post-compulsory training and, lastly, a more pronounced tendency to remain within the school system, thereby

Table 2.3   Overall number of young foreigners completing compulsory education and beginning occupational training (indices)

1976	Grade 9 N = 8,031 = 100	1977	Grade 10 in occupational training N = 7,466 = 100
1977	112	1978	115
1978	124	1979	126
1979	135	1980	134
1980	145	1981	143
1981	143	1982	147
1982	149	1983	158
1983	150	1984	–
1984	146	1985	–

Source: OFS, *Statistique des élèves* (various years).

deferring entry into working life when expected conditions do not materialize (CESDOC 1985: 19).

Surveys conducted by the authors within the FIPES project (Occupational Training and Integration of Young Foreigners and Swiss), in connection with the National Programme of Research into Occupational Training, enabled them to probe trends already apparent in this initial glimpse. The status of young people was analyzed, comparing the Swiss with the non-Swiss – chiefly Italians and Spaniards who are by far the most numerous of young foreigners residing in Switzerland. The field of study was restricted to three areas of the French-speaking part of the country which contain noticeable differences in their industrial base and labour market, yet which all have a large foreign population. Greater Geneva is characterized by a growing tertiary sector and employment capacity; however, owing to an influx of labour from other French-speaking areas and declining industrial output, its unemployment rate is about average (0.98 per cent in 1983). The western suburb of Lausanne is a sub-region where industry is fairly diversified; Vaud canton, in which it lies, enjoys relatively stable employment with a jobless rate (0.74 per cent) slightly below the national average. Finally, the Neuchâtel mountains area forming the characteristic Jurassian arc is devoted to a single industry, watch-making, in the canton hardest hit by unemployment (2.32 per cent) (Lewin 1983, cited by Feiburghaus 1985: 6).

In order to obtain a diachronical perspective, the authors surveyed two groups of young people: those having just completed compulsory

35

education (FIPES I) and another group, aged 25 to 27, already integrated for some time in the working world in so far as they hold a permanent-residence permit (FIPES III). Although it is obviously impossible to make a point-by-point comparison of the two sets of findings, the major trends can be highlighted. In the older group, the proportion of foreigners who never benefited from any post-compulsory training is easily triple (17 per cent) that of nationals in the same category (5 per cent), and the situation is particularly serious among immigrant women (29 per cent). Roughly 10 years later, those not having benefited from any post-compulsory training are far fewer (14 per cent and 11 per cent respectively for Swiss and non-Swiss), and the gap between foreign boys and girls has disappeared.

Obviously, initiating post-compulsory training is no guarantee of successful achievement of occupational skills which could be taken into account on the labour market. A study conducted in Geneva, which is due to be published shortly, reveals that a large number of apprenticeships are prematurely terminated, and by foreigners more so than by nationals (Swiss 45 per cent; Italians 54 per cent; and Spaniards 63 per cent). Although contract rescissions in most cases do not signify withdrawal from occupational training, they still point to occasionally ill-fated confrontations with the working world. In the FIPES research on young adults, it was noted that 11 per cent of Swiss and 18.5 per cent of foreigners did not manage to complete post-compulsory training (FIPES III 1985: 45).

Entry into working life: unemployment
Before delineating in greater detail how foreigners are present within post-compulsory training programmes, it is necessary to glance momentarily at the presence/absence of young people on the labour market. Employment rates will be compared by age bracket among the lowest range.

Being an alternative to training, employment tends – population-wise – to increase with age. In the 15- to 19-year age bracket, however, the lower employment rate of foreigners in comparison to nationals cannot be explained by their presence in vocational training programmes. Instead, it points to a greater difficulty integrating in the working world for both immigrant men and women. Only once, having overcome any notion of training, does the employment rate of foreigners equal, and even exceed, that of nationals. This situation is confirmed in unemployment statistics; the census reveals four times as many foreigners under 20 as Swiss seeking jobs.

The FIPES survey of young adults reveals roughly 4 per cent

Table 2.4 Employment rates of Swiss and non-Swiss residents by sex and age bracket, per cent

Age bracket (years)	Swiss			Non-Swiss		
	Total	Males	Females	Total	Males	Females
15–19	54.5	57.2	51.6	50.8	53.7	47.9
20–24	80.7	84.7	76.7	80.1	85.8	73.2
25–29	75.4	94.8	56.5	83.6	94.6	68.7

Source: OFS (1985).

seeking employment among both Swiss citizens and immigrants. However, the proportion of the unemployed drawing benefits and thus registered with unemployment insurance agencies stands lower, at around 2 per cent, yet double the country's average unemployment rate for 1983: 0.9 per cent. The jobless seem to have a below-average occupational training level and often reside in the Neuchâtel mountains area, hardest hit by recession. These findings may have only relative signifiance, given the limited number of people surveyed (FIPES III 1985: 125–7).

In the areas under study at least, young foreigners do not appear to be more greatly affected by unemployment than their Swiss counterparts. It should be pointed out, however, that this situation may be due in part to the departure of a sizable segment of the immigrant population in the mid-70s.

Access to occupational training: qualitative aspects
It has been noted that most young foreigners now leaving compulsory education are enrolled in post-compulsory training programmes. In 1980, Italians and Spaniards accounted for 5.8 per cent of those engaged in this level of training but were under-represented in junior college (4.5 per cent) and slightly over-represented in occupational training (OFS, *Statistique des élèves* 1980–81).

Based on the longitudinal survey of cohorts conducted in Zurich, a complete comparison may be drawn between the differential integration patterns of Swiss and non-Swiss youth. Here, a cross-section of Swiss citizens born in 1963 is viewed alongside young Italians of the same age living in Zurich (Italians make up 50 per cent of all young foreigners) (Gurny *et al.* 1984). This is one of the largest groups of cohorts to arrive on the labour market as it

| | Italians | | Swiss | |
	Males	Females	Males	Females
Attending school				
Swiss senior secondary	39	46	36	47
Italian senior secondary	4	5		
Swiss junior secondary	10	6	21	17
Total	53	57	57	64
Beginning working life				
Doing an apprenticeship	23	11	36	26
Taking elementary training	17	18	4	5
Employed without training	4	11	1	–
No information available	3	3	1	6
Total	47	43	42	37
N =	162	150	236	224

Source: Gurny *et al.* (1984).

was moving towards recession. Table 2.5 shows their situation at the age of 16.

The social status of Swiss citizens and foreigners differs sharply as regards entry into the working world. In particular, the proportion of those taking scaled-down training (elementary or on-the-job training) or having no training whatsoever is four times higher among Italian males than Swiss males (21 per cent as opposed to 5 per cent) and even six times higher among female immigrants (29 per cent as opposed to 5 per cent).

Thus, although the overall percentage of elementary training contracts remains limited, it should be realized that foreigners are especially vulnerable to the risks incurred by training that does not lead to official recognition. For example, the government Message accompanying the Occupational Training Bill currently in force listed the trade 'sawyer of materials'. This situation is clearly not the outcome of chance. In the same Message, the government strove for the institutionalization of this type of training, saying:

It may be considered that the steps taken in view of restricting the number of alien workers, coupled with the structural difficulties encountered in certain economic sectors, will result in greater use of indigenous labour with elementary training. (Conseil Fédéral 1977: 43)

FIPES I research gives a more in-depth view of different types of training, especially apprenticeships in business and industry. Three major factors dictate the occupational fate of young people: social background, sex and nationality. It has been observed that, while the large majority of foreign males (79 per cent) prepare for manual trades in the secondary sector, this is true of only 45 per cent of their Swiss cohorts.

Foremost on the list of occupations pursued by foreign males are auto and auto-body mechanic, electrician-fitter and auto painter, whereas Swiss males most frequently settle into white-collar jobs or become salesmen, cooks and carpenters (FIPES I 1984: 101). By contrast, none of the girls interviewed was learning a trade in the secondary sector; the trend towards service industries is easily visible and probably exaggerated by dwindling secondary employment in the areas under study. Yet this common fate does not necessarily wipe away discrepancies. While over a quarter of female immigrants learn a trade in hairdressing or body care, not one Swiss girl in the survey was oriented towards these occupations. Most were to become office workers and sales clerks.

Furthermore, 90 per cent of the foreign apprentices surveyed worked alongside other non-Swiss staff, as opposed to 65 per cent of their Swiss counterparts. The social environment of the two groups thus tends to be different. Based on the fact that most young foreigners work in firms where over 25 per cent of the employees are non-Swiss, it can be legitimately inferred that there are pockets of immigrant labour where first and second generations mingle (ibid.: 126).

A recent Geneva-based study on annual occupational training enrolment by canton attempted to analyze the educational standard of apprentices in a number of these occupations. Although the findings hinge in part on the idiosyncrasies of the school system in question, they help delineate certain factors within the respective status of these occupations. Some 70 per cent of apprentice mechanics and hairdressers, for example, are recruited from junior secondary schools (26 per cent of hairdressers even left compulsory schooling at the minimum legal age while not having successfully completed the curriculum). The remaining 30 per cent are divided into those who continued their training in a post-compulsory programme prior to finding a job or beginning an apprenticeship, and those whose educational background could not be determined.

In other occupations, such as salesman or office worker, this

Table 2.6 Post-compulsory training standards reached by 25-year-old adults based on nationality, per cent

	Swiss	Non-Swiss
Further education	18	7
Occupational training	65	56
No post-compulsory qualifications	16	35
No information available	1	1
N =	210	325

Source: FIPES III (1985), 45.

proportion dwindles to 50 per cent and 37 per cent respectively. This prompted Amos (1984: 99) to conclude that the 'now ingrained distinction between white- and blue-collar workers seems to gain a measure of relevance at the beginning of an apprenticeship'.

Based on findings such as these, it can be asserted that foreigners tend to be more numerous in apprenticeships where lower educational standards prevail, reflecting lower entrance requirements. Some 80 per cent of non-Swiss apprentices in the FIPES I survey entered programmes having compulsory education requirements termed 'elementary', as opposed to 60 per cent of Swiss apprentices (FIPES I 1984: 105).

Not everyone who begins a training programme completes it. This is especially clear judging from the FIPES III survey of adults aged 25 to 27. Here, of course, entrance requirements in force ten years ago, in 1973–74, are being referred to. Low standards were much more frequent among the adults surveyed than might have been expected by transposing statistics on entry into post-compulsory training by younger people.

Similar proportions of Swiss males and females are 'unskilled', largely owing to non-completion of a training programme, although unskilled female immigrants outnumber males by 43 per cent to 29 per cent. Most unskilled females (28 per cent of those surveyed) never began post-compulsory training, whereas most unskilled males (23 per cent of those surveyed) were either unable or did not manage to complete their training successfully. The deferred immigration of most women (coupled with its corollaries: education in their native country and greater difficulties in transferrring to occupational-training programmes in the host country) partially explains this outcome. Although dampened, it persists, even when only those children who arrived in Switzerland at pre-selection age (before 10 years old) are considered. Finally, given equal education, the qualifications of young people no longer differ according to nationality: the impact on occupational integration of social background is deflected by compulsory education. The breakdown of occupational skills is reflected in the type of job fulfilled: while the majority of foreign males engaged in manual trades (69 per cent) are thus mainly blue-collar workers, most of their Swiss cohorts are white-collar workers (54 per cent).

Although it points to differing patterns, the polarization in women's jobs is equally pronounced. More immigrant women, for example, are employed (68 per cent as opposed to 61 per cent), especially married women (63 per cent as opposed to 46 per cent). Moreover, jobs held by Swiss women are concentrated (more so than for men) in middle- and upper-strata occupations (73 per cent). Foreign women, meanwhile, are divided between two types of social status: in jobs similar to those held by Swiss women (46 per cent); and in manual jobs usually requiring no special skills (43 per cent). Their occupational status strongly resembles that of their mothers before them.

Completion of occupational training does not necessarily grant access to a job requiring special skills. Some 10 to 12 per cent of those surveyed were unable to market their skills and therefore occupied unskilled positions. Under-employment affects women much more than men; it almost doubles in the case of nationals (8 per cent for men, 14 per cent for women). This discrepancy between occupational skills and the jobs young people find more than triples for foreigners (7 per cent for men and 25 per cent for women) (FIPES III 1985: 89). Non-Swiss women, therefore, encounter two kinds of hurdles in their socio-occupational integration: firstly, in access to training (a difficulty that tends to diminish to the extent that it is linked to migrant status), and secondly, in the return on their investment in occupational training, that is, the opportunity of ultimately finding a job using their skills. It is not yet possible to evaluate the development of this predicament; local observers tend to indicate its persistence ten years later.

Mobility and its particular patterns among the immigrant population

Geographical mobility versus territorial roots: the settlement of migrant workers
One of the great advantages in hiring foreign workers has lain in

their extreme flexibility and ability to adapt quickly to changes in the demand for labour, changes caused chiefly by seasonal and economic variations, but also by geographic and sectorial considerations. Spurred by this realization of their mobility, the tendency emerged to attribute these 'qualities' to immigrants themselves and depict migrant workers as the epitome of *homo oeconomicus* of time-honoured tradition. Set adrift from the social web linking them to their original milieu, their transition from adolescence to adulthood broken by the absence of a peer group and family, immigrants are uprooted and so must bend to economic pressure.

While not denying the grounds for this interpretation, the authors prefer to explain the mobility of immigrant labour by the policies for controlling the stream of foreign workers, which have closely guided provisions for this portion of the supply of labour. The measures have notably included rotation and administrative restrictions governing place of residence and work.

If this interpretation is accurate, the maturing of a migration stream (Böhning 1974), which encompasses an increased number of both permanent-residence permit holders whose situation is not controlled and young people having lived most, if not all, of their lives in the 'host' country, is tending gradually to negate the circumstances at the root of the distributive mobility of foreigners. Lesser geographic mobility must therefore be expected on the part of second-generation immigrants in comparison with their parents. Comparison of national statistics reveals that immigrants are one-third less mobile than Swiss workers (Schuler, in Brugger 1985). More accurately stated, lesser mobility is found among the young adults surveyed (FIPES III 1985).

Foreigners appear more resistant than nationals to geographical mobility for reasons of employment opportunities and less inclined to leave their 'home away from home' to pursue or complete their training. Mobility for personal reasons is more pronounced however, prompting more foreign women (50 per cent) than men (39 per cent) to move. Within one area only – the Neuchâtel mountains – does the behaviour of nationals and foreigners differ. There, the foreigners, that is the less skilled workers, seem to find more jobs than the Swiss, who are more willing to commute to the cantonal capital. Overall, in business and office work, twice as many nationals as foreigners (78 per cent to 35 per cent) are affected by mobility; in the technical trades, the proportion is one and a half times higher (44 per cent to 30 per cent).

The end of the out-and-out *homo oeconomicus* status of migrant workers is also confirmed in the FIPES survey by the greater reluctance of foreigners to envisage moving solely to earn a higher

Table 2.7 Motives and geographical mobility based on nationality, per cent

	Swiss	Non-Swiss
Reasons for mobility		
Work	32	18
Training	14	11
Other reasons	11	17
Total mobility	57	46
No mobility	42	55
N =	210	325

Source: FIPES III (1985), 128.

salary. Wage differentials no longer wield the immediate power they did in the 1960s over distributive mobility (Maillat 1968). It is only towards foreign lands that immigrants show a greater inclination to move than nationals, and their purpose in doing so is practically irrelevant.

There is one further indicator of how foreigners are becoming partially settled in local labour markets. The distribution of Swiss and non-Swiss workers by economic sector does not differ appreciably within a given region; the employment rate of foreigners, however, does deviate from one region to the next, underscoring disparities in the local supply of labour. While jobs held by the first generation largely bore an ethnic imprint, those held by the second combine regional idiosyncrasies and the persistence of a certain national differentiation.

Self-employment versus waged labour
Several European studies, carried out notably in France, highlight the very intriguing development of an industrial web of small businesses directed by immigrants, generally of the second or third generation (Instituto F. Santi 1983: 61), and mostly operating in the traditionally immigrant sectors of employment, such as construction and tailoring. In Switzerland, the situation is different. This is due on one hand to the less residential seniority amongst immigrants (a permanent-residence permit is required for operating a business), and on the other hand to the economic structure of the

country, which tends to concentrate on medium-scale corporate enterprises.

The FIPES survey, however, which to the authors' knowledge was the first to explore this issue, revealed a significant proportion of young people in business for themselves. Indeed, foreigners harbour such plans much more often than do nationals: 51 per cent as opposed to 28 per cent among apprentices in the survey (FIPES I 1984: 117). However, the proportion of self-employed people, that is of young people who actually managed to attain their goal, is identical: 7 per cent at the age of 25 to 27 (FIPES III 1985: 96). A curious reversal in trend can be noted among the self-employed in relation to wage-earners: Swiss 'employers' lean towards the trades sector, while foreigners tend to work in the services, mainly as small tradesmen. These businesses are not inherited from the family; none of the self-employed came from a family of businessmen or worked at the same occupation as his parents, at least not the occupation he held upon emigration. Instead, these business ventures can be interpreted as a pursual of social mobility, a strategy traditionally used by the working class. They are also the most common objective of migration, the goal for which many emigrants are willing to make sacrifices.

Mobility on the labour market

Social mobility can be understood to be the route individuals and groups follow within a socially structured space. It is the result of the interaction of individual actors – their behaviour and strategies – within the social structures which organize inequality into a hierarchy of well-defined positions. In this way the authors came to consider vertical mobility to be more significant than horizontal mobility (for example whether it be across economic sectors or geographic). Although the latter may possibly be related to vertical mobility, it holds less strategic importance.

In focusing the study on the status of youth, the authors were first of all led to explore the inter-generational perspective. Its relevance lies in the fact that analysis of the relative position of those who could be designated as the first generation within the stratification system displayed very specific patterns. Here it might suffice to refer to the process of *Unterschichtung* (the creation of an underclass) identified by Hoffmann-Nowotny (1973) with respect to the integration of foreign workers in the social structure in the host country – in this case Switzerland.

The study was undertaken knowing full well that the data would not allow an accurate account for the age consequence. Only those individuals nearing the end of their working lives (fathers) could

Table 2.8   Inter-generational mobility of Swiss males

| Occupational status | Sons | | | | Total |
| | Blue collar | | White collar | | |
	N	%	N	%	N, fathers
Fathers					
Blue collar	19	50	21	46	40
White collar	19	50	25	54	44
Total					
N, sons	38	100	46	100	84

N = number of cases
Source: FIPES III (1985), 78.

be compared with those who had recently begun theirs (their children). The mobility that can be reported on, therefore, does not lend full credence to the impact of intra-generational mobility, which, as is well known, was especially frequent among the fathers' generation. Although these considerations call for caution, they do not negate the relevance of studying this perspective, for the study reveals the beginning of the process.

Moreover, if the findings are split (because of the small number of subjects), the variable socio-occupational category is reduced to the 'blue collar' – 'white collar' dimension. The dividing line between them remains relatively clear; that is intra-generational mobility tends to be rather difficult.

A comparison of the totals in Table 2.8 reveals a remarkably stable employment structure among the Swiss (blue-collar workers range from 48 per cent to 45 per cent). By contrast, manual labour among immigrants is in sharp decline (roughly 10 per cent, since it drops from 86 per cent to 78 per cent), even while remaining largely predominant. Self-recruitment is higher among foreigners (67 per cent) than is the case for nationals (52 per cent).

The mobility of the working women surveyed, as compared with their original social status, brings to light more pronounced structural changes than in the case of men. The lower stratum is clearly diminishing in size, possibly owing partly to differences in the nature of men's and women's work. The reduction has reached 50 per cent in the case of Swiss women and, although proportionally smaller, is also large among immigrant women (37 per cent) (see appendix).

Social mobility may be better grasped by comparing the socio-

Table 2.9   Inter-generational mobility of foreign males

| Occupational status | Sons Blue collar | | White collar | | Total |
	N	%	N	%	N, fathers
Fathers					
Blue collar	73	78	29	81	102
White collar	10	22	7	19	17
Total					
N, sons	93	100	36	100	119

N = Number of cases
Source: FIPES III. (1985), 79.

Table 2.10   Social stratum of workers of lower social milieu based on nationality, per cent

	Swiss	Non-Swiss
Lower stratum	42	62.6
Middle and upper strata	58	37.4
N =	64	163.0

Source: FIPES III. (1985), 81.

occupational integration of young people having a similar social background. In other words, the question may be posed as to whether the observed stratification based on nationality reflects the well-known stratification found among immigrant workers of the first generation. Most often, the sons and daughters of foreign manual labourers are allegedly reduced to the plain and simple reproduction of social classes. Yet this reproduction operates differently among young Swiss adults and their foreign counterparts: the latter's mobility is more limited than the former's. In other words, the child of a foreign manual or unskilled worker stands a reduced chance of rising to the middle and upper strata than a Swiss child of similar station.

While social mobility is a reality for a small number of young Swiss from the lower stratum, the majority of immigrant workers' children remain in the lower stratum to which their parents belong.

Closer scrutiny of social mobility, taking into consideration employment skills within the lower stratum, reveals that, of all nationality and sex categories, foreign women of lower milieu most often end up in the lower skilled stratum. Meanwhile, Swiss citizens of similar background, both male and female, are distributed more or less like their parents among the various social strata. Thus, sex is a secondary factor of discrimination, significant only once the primary discriminatory factor (nationality) has already taken effect.

The differentiated reproduction of the lower stratum takes the form of a generally lower socio-occupational status for foreigners than for young Swiss adults. The former's low social mobility stems, in particular, from a lower standard of post-compulsory training. Differences in training, especially occupational training, serve as the direct cause of – and justification for – their lower status. The reason why they are relegated to this lower socio-occupational station is that they are not granted an equal chance, and their inferior training causes this status to be viewed as normal, that is as complying with an individualistic and merit-based conception of social mobility. In other words, it is not because they are foreigners that most of them are destined to remain unskilled labourers. Rather, being foreigners and the sons of labourers (the latter not synonymous with the former), they do not achieve the same skill level as the average young Swiss adult.

This type of legitimation is all the more likely in the case of foreign men, to the extent that most manage to complete officially recognized post-compulsory training. This was not true of their fathers, and thus most – and in a proportion similar to that of Swiss men – secure skilled jobs. Undoubtedly, this limited social mobility of the lower stratum is valued both by Swiss institutions and coincides with the aspirations of their parent's generation.

Foreign women appear much less apt to justify their status in relation to training and occupational integration. They are not only victim to systematic inequalities befalling the category of young foreign adults (lower socio-occupational status, more limited social mobility, inferior training standard and greater vulnerability to educational competition); it is most often they who suffer from de-qualification.

While it would be inaccurate to say that foreigners keep on being labourers from generation to generation, as is the case in other settings, the fact is that boys usually follow their fathers' footsteps, as so often do girls. Unlike young Swiss adults who chiefly belong to the middle and upper strata, the children of immigrant workers who came from southern Europe largely remain in the lower class. In so doing, they contribute to the reproduction of the working class in Switzerland, a class that is dwindling in both relative and absolute terms as a result of evolution towards a a post-industrial society.

Occupational goals and the objectives of young foreigners

Studies of immigrants in Switzerland tend to overlook the immigrants' own concept of their situation and the strategies they implement in their relations with the host country, in both a vital and a practical respect. Because of this, it is possible to quote only certain incomplete data taken from the FIPES survey. Unfortunately the authors were unable to complete and expand upon this information themselves, and can therefore draw no conclusions on the training system and labour market and the motivating forces of the young people themselves.

Attempts have often been made to find an explanation for the differing status of immigrants and nationals in the two groups' cultural characteristics. The study by Strodtbeck *et al.* (1957) is a prime example. Without really being able to investigate this type of conception, the authors have nevertheless endeavoured to challenge certain common-sense notions which, in their view, are offshoots of this tendency. Such is the debate over 'mentalities', by which it is argued, for instance, that immigrants are less successful because they place less value on training and work. This is a way of making the 'victims' responsible for their own fate.

The fact is that half the young people polled in the FIPES I survey claim that what their parents desire above all for their future is that they pursue senior secondary training. This is practically a constant, regardless of nationality: 50 per cent of the non-Swiss parents actually tend to be more ambitious than the Swiss, especially where their sons are concerned. Overall, however, the non-Swiss remain fairly realistic, that is capable of changing these plans considerably depending on their offsprings' educational achievements. Moreover attitudes of 25 year olds towards work were analyzed and whether these attitudes fell into an instrumental or a more expressive category. Here it was discovered that attitudes were polarized not according to nationality but according to types of occupation. The issue of identificational behaviour must therefore be raised, not only with regard to nationality, but also to socio-occupational status and training programme.

Research into the socialization and identity of young foreigners often uses the most visible factor – age at migration – as a variable for explaining social profile. This is done, for example, by Schrader *et al.* (1976). Such studies ultimately propose mechanistic integration models, where both variations in social status – real (although limited in the case of migrants from southern Europe) and, more generally, sub-cultural variations, found in both the foreign and host societies – are overlooked. It was the desire to grasp the multifold nature of these influences that prompted the authors to do a factoral analysis of correspondence. Interesting statistical relationships were observed: firstly between the social and educational dimensions of migrants; and, secondly, between a number of behaviour patterns within society seen as the indicators of identity. These procedures are linked to two institutionalized referents of national background: spoken language and nationality (Oriol 1979).

Three types of young foreigners are highlighted in Figure 2.1. In the left half is someone who is himself an immigrant; born in his native country, he arrived in Switzerland at a variable age (school age farthest left). He is further defined by the use of his native language (NL) with his brothers and sisters (decisions concerning belongingness do not appear). This type of immigrant may be considered someone who bears the imprint of the society of origin in migratory circumstances. In short, he has a migrant identity.

In the upper right-hand corner, another type appears whose behaviour and strategies are characterized by invisibility. He speaks only French at home, rejects the idea of return to the country of origin and entertains the prospect of naturalization. Such identificational behaviour is synonymous with middle- or upper-class origins, a demanding educational programme and attendance at business college. This type of strategy, therefore, seems linked to a high socio-cultural standard, although these findings are not sufficient to enable the reader to establish a cause-and-effect relationship in either direction.

In the lower right-hand corner, yet another type appears, in sharp contrast with the previous ones. He is characterized by the practice of bilingualism (French and native language) with his parents, a refusal to become naturalized and uncertainty over his 'return'. People of this type encountered only basic educational requirements, attended private schools, did an apprenticeship, originated from a lower social class and were born in Switzerland. This type might be considered as someone who embodies two sets of references; socialization to life in Switzerland has not erased cultural traits from his country of origin. His uncertainty over 'returning home' appears particularly significant, and the term 'return' is itself inappropriate since his whole life has been spent in Switzerland.

It should be emphasized that language patterns are clearly related to attitudes towards return and naturalization. Young people who are thinking about returning home – and who are not considering acquiring Swiss nationality – continue to use their native language.

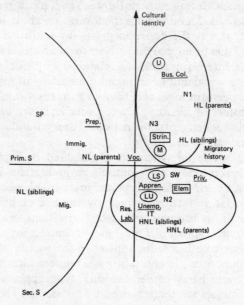

Figure 2.1 *Three types of cultural identity (analysis of correspondences)*

Source: FIPES I (1984), 228.

Key

Country of birth:	Born SW	Born in Switzerland		Priv.	Private vocational school
	Born IT.	Born in Italy		Voc.	Full-time vocational school
	Born SP.	Born in Spain			
Migratory history:	None	Born and raised in Switzerland		Prep.	Preparatory school
	Res.	Always lived in Switzerland	Father's social stratum:	Bus. Col.	Business college.
				U	Upper
				M	Middle
	Immig.	Born and raised in It/Sp, then moved to Switzerland		LS	Lower skilled
				L UN	Lower unskilled
	Mig.	Lived successively in Switzerland, It/Sp and Switzerland.	Education:	Elem	Elementary requirements
				Strin	More stringent requirements
	Others			Elem I/S	Elementary partially in It/Sp
Education upon arrival:	Arrival	All education in Switzerland		M Strin I/S	More stringent Partially in It/Sp
	Prim. S.	Arrived in Switzerland at primary school age	Language spoken with father, mother and siblings (3 variables):	HL	Host language (French)
	Sec. S.	Arrived in Switzerland at secondary school age		NL	Native language (Italian or Spanish)
	Rotation	Repeated migration		HNL	French and Italian/ Spanish
Current occupation:	Lab.	Unskilled labour	Naturaliza- tion plans:	N1	Yes
	Unemp.	Not gainfully employed		N2	No
	Apprent.	Apprenticeship		N3	Undecided

50

However those who plan to be naturalized use French at home. In contrast to the 'migrant' type, who is characterized by his ties with the country of origin but who does not have a specific occupational profile, two clusters of young people are found who have lived their entire lives in Switzerland. Both are defined by specific identificational behaviour, social background and training: (a) a strategy of social invisibility for children of the middle and upper classes with a higher educational and occupational level (especially business college); and (b) strategies of dual references for children of the lower class with a lower educational and occupational level, often apprentices, private school pupils or those having no formal training.

The development of this latter type seems to confirm the 'bilaterality of references' (Catani 1983: 35) of migrants: as a way of living an international dimension, which goes beyond the present usual conceptualizations. The bilaterality of references is a way of refusing national belongingness as the only or exclusive alternative. Instead life is experienced as something where both generational continuity and a permanent anchorage in the every-day reality of the new country may be interwoven.

The co-presence of these last two types casts doubt on the validity of applying unilinear models of integration. While language habits and symbolic choices of the first type indicate a tendency to adopt behaviour similar to the dominant cultural practices of the host country, the same is not true of the second type. This one has retained links with his parents' culture of origin before and during emigration. It is as if this type, who represents the majority of the people surveyed, were the expression of a partially reproduced and ethnically identifiable fraction of the lower stratum. This identification, however, concerns individualized choices and habits lived in a private sphere, which are not accompanied – at least as things now stand – either by forms of socio-economic marginalization or of socio-political mobilization.

A summary: macro-social factors influencing the integration of young foreigners

The socio-occupational status of young foreigners, as it appears in this study, may come as a suprise when compared with the prevailing situation in other countries. To appreciate the actual scope of these findings, the reader should bear in mind both the problems and methodological idiosyncrasies of the authors' research, along with the specific macro-social patterns of the Swiss context.

This study centred on a certain category of young foreigners –

the majority – whose right to reside at some length in Switzerland has been either officially or unofficially recognized. As a result, the less secure portion of young foreigners was excluded from the surveys, that is young people who only later were able to join their fathers, together with illegal immigrant children (whose parents' status does not allow them to join their fathers). Obviously, this group has a high failure rate at school and in occupational training. Socially speaking, however, it remains out of view, as it escapes statistical detection.

Surveys such as this one can only approach reality at a micro-social level. Despite this, it is not possible to be content with seeking explanations for tendencies observed only at this level. This is one of the major criticisms the authors have against a great deal of migration research. Basic insights are to be found in macro-social factors. As it happens, the situation of young foreigners in Switzerland seems largely pre-determined by three main factors: demographic change; immigration policy; and the labour-market situation. These factors are obviously interdependent in many ways and apt to hinge in turn on conditions that go beyond the framework of this chapter and which it is not possible to examine at this time.

The unemployment rate among young foreigners – higher than the national average, yet very low in comparison with that of other European countries – only points to the absence of large-scale unemployment and of a political and social debate over the nature of existing unemployment. The absence of large-scale unemployment is, in turn, partially due to the change in the supply of labour, which has witnessed a sharp reduction in the employment level of permanent resident (Swiss and non-Swiss) from 72 per cent in 1973 to 65 per cent in 1983 (OECD 1985: 47). It is also due to immigration policy (during both the 1975–76 and 1982–83 recessions, the decrease in the number of non-permanent foreigners accounted for 75 per cent and 45 per cent respectively of jobs lost) (ibid.: 44).

It is therefore impossible for the fluctuating portion of the foreign population which, as has been seen, accounts for roughly one-third of foreign workers to 'give birth to' a second generation of immigrants resident in Switzerland. This reduces correspondingly the number of young people apt to suffer from adaptation problems.

Demography has a multiple impact on the status of young foreigners. What was frequently presented as exporting unemployment or, at least, reducing foreign labour led to the return home of family groups, thereby shrinking the number of the second generation. The most noticeable effect of this was slackened demand for occupational training at a time when the labour market was being swamped by large terminal classes. On a longer-term basis, the declining birth rate 'reduces' demand for training as opposed to its supply, so much so that nowadays frontier commuters are being allowed to do apprenticeships. Finally, another major demographic factor – necessarily overlooked in micro-sociological approaches – is the relatively high proportion of young foreigners. In Switzerland, foreigners comprise over 14 per cent in corresponding 15 to 19 year old age brackets, as opposed to about 7 per cent in France and West Germany, the two neighbouring countries with which it is always compared in respect of immigration. The greater share of young foreigners in this age bracket in Switzerland could make it more difficult to marginalize them. This most probably diversifies the social status of young foreigners, thereby raising the average standard on which comparisons are ordinarily based.

Lastly, the impact that the procedures for acquiring nationality have on the social perception and statistical illustration of the second generation, on which all studies necessarily depend, should be stressed again. While it is possible to define the second generation in different ways, the only quantitative indicator is nationality. Automatic processes of naturalization are geared to preserve the original nationality only of the most unstable portion of the foreign population. By contrast, very selective naturalization processes, such as those in force in Switzerland, go on perpetuating the political and legal exclusion of the second – and already the third – generations which have preserved their foreign nationality.

This just proves that mere comparisons of international statistics can be completely misleading!

Appendix

Table 2.A1   Inter-generational mobility of Swiss females

Occupational status	Daughters				
	Blue collar		White collar		Total
	N	%	N	%	N, fathers
Fathers					
Blue collar	8	67	16	46	24
White collar	4	33	19	54	23
Total					
N, daughters	12	100	35	100	47

N = number of cases
Source: FIPES III. (1985), 79.

Table 2.A2   *Inter-generational mobility of immigrant females*

| Occupational status | Daughters Blue collar | | White collar | | Total |
	N	%	N	%	N, fathers
Fathers					
Blue collar	30	77	32	89	62
White collar	9	23	4	11	13
Total					
N, daughters	39	100	36	100	75

N = number of cases
Source: FIPES III. (1985), 79.

References

Abrahamsen, Y., Kaplanek H. & Schips B. (1986), *Arbeitsmarkttheorie, Arbeitsmarktpolitik und Beschäftigung in der Schweiz*, Gruesch: Ruegger.

Amos, J. (1984), 'L'entrée en apprentissage. Capital scolaire et marché de l'apprentissage à Genève' (1970–1981), *Cahiers du Service de la Recherche Sociologique*, **20**, Geneva.

Böhning, W. R. (1974), 'Les conséquences économiques de l'emploi des travailleurs étrangers concernant en particulier les marchés du travail des pays de l'Europe Occidentale' in OECD, *Les Effets de l'Emploi des Travailleurs Etrangers*, Paris: OECD.

Brugger, E. A. (1985), *Développement Économique Régional*, Lausanne: Presses Polytechniques Romandes.

Catani, M. (1983), 'Une hypothèse de lecture des relations entre parents et enfants: émigration, individualisation et réversibilité orientée des choix', in *Identité et Culture: Hypothèses Théoriques et Perspectives Interdisciplinaires dans l'Etude des Communautés Italiennes en France*, Paris, rapport intermédiaire au CNRS.

CESDOC (Centre Suisse de Documentation en Matière d'Enseignement et d'Éducation) (1985), *Demain . . . combien d'élèves?*, Conférence Suisse des Directeurs Cantonaux de l'Instruction Publique et Office Fédérale de la Statistique, Gd Saconnex.

Commission pour les questions conjoncturelles (1986), *La Théorie et la Politique du Marché du Travail et de l'Emploi en Suisse*. 300th bulletin, (Supplement to *La Vie Économique*, April).

Conseil Fédéral (1977) *Message Concernant une Nouvelle Loi Fédérale sur la Formation Professionnelle*, Bern, 26 February.

Département Fédéral de l'Economie Publique, *La Vie Économique*, Bern, monthly issues

FIPES I (1984), de Rham, G., Fibbi, R., and Virnot, O., 'L'entrée dans la formation professionnelle. Rapport de recherche sur la formation et l'insertion professionnelle des jeunes étrangers et Suisses', Programme national de recherche 'Education et vie active', mimeo, Lausanne and Geneva.

FIPES III (1985), Fibbi, R., Virnot, O., and de Rham, G., 'Différenciation sociale et reproduction des appartenances. Rapport de recherche sur la formation et l'insertion professionnelle des jeunes étrangers et Suisses', Programme national de recherche 'Education et vie active', mimeo, Lausanne and Geneva.

Freiburghaus, D. (1985), 'Entstehung neuer Fronten auf dem schweizerischen Arbeitsmarkt' Schweizer Wissenschaftsrat, *Forschungspolititsche Früherkennung*, **8**, Bern.

Gurny, R., Cassee, P., Hausser, H. P., and Meyer, A. (1984), *Karrieren und Sackgassen*, Diessenhofen: Verlag Ruegger.

Hoffmann-Nowotny, H. J. (1973), *Soziologie des Fremdarbeiterproblems*, Stuttgart, Enke Verlag.

Hug, K. (1986), 'Situation et perspectives du marché suisse du travail et points saillants de la politique relative au marché de l'emploi', *La Vie Économique*, January, 1–15.

Hutmacher, W. (1981), 'Migrations, production et reproduction de la société', in A. Gretler, R. Gurny, A. N. Perret-Clermont, and E. Poglia, *Etre Migrant*, Bern: P. Lang.

Instituto F. Santi (1983), *Le 'Comunità' ed i gruppi d'emigrati italiani in Francia. Verso un nuovo modello di relazioni tra l'emigrazione e le zone d'origine*, Rome.

Maillat, D. (1968) *Structure des Salaires et Immigration*, Neuchâtel: La Baconnière.

Maillat, D. (1974), 'Les effets économiques de l'emploi des travailleurs étrangers: le cas suisse', in OECD, *Les Effets de l'Emploi des Travailleurs Étrangers*, Paris: OECD.

OECD (1985), *Suisse/Switzerland*, Paris.

OFIAMT (Office Fédéral de l'industrie, des Arts et Métiers et du Travail) (1980), *Politique Concernant le Marché du Travail en Suisse: Caractéristiques et Problèmes*.

OFS (Office Fédéral de la Statistique) (1985) *Recensement Fédéral de la Population 1980 (RP)*, Bern: OFS.

OFS (Office Fédéral de la Statistique), *Statistique des Élèves*, Bern, various years.

Oriol, M. (1979), 'Identité produite, instituée, exprimée', *Cahiers Internationaux de Sociologie*, **LXVI**.

Piore, M. (1973), 'Fragments of a sociological theory of wages', *American Economic Review*, **63**, May.

Schrader, A., Nikles, B. W. and Griese, H. M. (1976), *Die Zweite Generation. Sozialisation und Akkulturation ausländischer Kinder in der Bundesrepublik*, Dronberg: Athenäum Verlag.

Schuler, M. (1984), 'Ausländerpolitik und Mobilität der Ausländer in der Schweiz', in E. A. Brugger, (ed.), *Arbeitsmarktentwicklung: Schicksalsfrage der Regionalpolitik?*, Diessenhofen: Verlag Rüegger.

Strodtbeck, F. L., McDonald, M. C., and Rosen, B. C. (1957), 'Evaluation of Occupations: A Reflection of Jewish and Italian Mobility Differences', *American Sociological Review*, **XXII**, 546–53.

Weiss, P., (1986) *La Mobilité Sociale*, Paris: Presses Universitaires de France (Que Sais-Je?").

3   Ethnic Minority Youth in a Collapsing Labour Market: The UK Experience

Malcolm Cross

Introduction

This chapter will argue that ethnic minorities have unwittingly become involved in a massive transformation of the British economy which has turned the story of migration on its head. The vast majority of the UK's Asian and Afro-Caribbean population either migrated for work, or are descended from those who came for that reason. They went to areas of low unemployment and relatively high wages, accepting in the process that they would come to occupy positions unwanted by the indigenous working class, even if this meant working well below their level of skill and experience. Since then the areas of ethnic minority concentration have been profoundly affected by the collapse in employment, as economic restructuring, following in the wake of the European recession, has radically altered the topography of the labour market. Their options for moving again are now radically reduced, both internally and externally. Of paramount importance is the virtual disappearance in some local labour markets of the opportunity to work. The original enterprise to migrate is being replaced by a sense of place, producing for some a 'reservation' identity in which the safety and friendliness of the known is preferred to the discrimination and hostility of the wider society. The original autonomy and independence of migrants is being replaced in the so-called 'second generation' by a new dependency on the family and on the state. Remarkably, the will to work and to gain skill and further education appear to have survived, but training policy has not sought to capture the creativity associated with those of recent migrant origin. Instead it has tended to be based on the judgment that declines in employment are evidence of lowered levels of employability.

In defending this analysis, the recent transition in the UK labour market as a whole will first be looked at, concentrating in particular on its spatial effects. The same section will also examine the general features of labour market policy. This will be followed by consideration of ethnic minorities themselves in terms of their position in this changing labour market. Training policy will then be examined once again, but this time in relation to minorities. Finally, the consequences of labour-market location and public policy for mobility, both occupational and geographical, will be considered. The overall conclusion is that it is increasingly necessary to recognize the difference between the Asian and Afro-Carribean experience, where the former have gained some occupational success unaided by labour-market policy, while the latter are experiencing profound difficulties, unhelped – and possibly even hindered – by policy intervention.

The labour market and public policy

Throughout the 1950s and 1960s, which was the period when the UK acquired ethnic minority communities of any size, the economic policy of both major parties was dominated by a Keynesian consensus. The central issue was judged to be demand-management, with deficit budgeting in trade-cycle lows and tax increases and 'prices and incomes' policies at the peaks of economic activity. Economic problems were defined in terms of avoiding the cessation of post-war growth in the former period and of achieving acceptable rates of inflation in the latter. In both periods, the international reserves and currency values figured prominently in the economic calculus of each successive government. Supply-side thinking was conspicuous by its absence, and never more clearly so than in the unregulated and unmonitored admission of migrants from the West Indies and, later, from the Indian sub-continent. By the late 1970s, the consensus broke down, as it did in many advanced industrial countries, when it became clear that demand-management alone, in the face of fierce international competition from newly emerging industrial countries, could not guarantee the efficiency necessary to sustain continued economic growth.

The labour market transition

Declines in real growth rates, coupled with an ever-increasing pace of technological change, produced a transition in the labour market, which had two major features. Firstly, there was a decline in the demand for labour and, secondly, a shift in demand from full-time unskilled and semi-skilled jobs in manufacturing to employment in the 'new service' sector, much of it part-time. Coupled with this transition has come a new geography of employment (Massey 1984). New employment opportunities have not kept pace with declines in areas of traditional manufacturing employment. Where the service sector has always been strong, it has tended to grow stronger, supplemented by new areas of employment concentration, often in small towns and cities least affected by the manufacturing-based industrial revolution of the last century. The implications for ethnic minorities are profound. They were the final injection of labour power into the declining industries: a last ditch attempt in the battle to regain competitiveness by incorporating low-cost labour. The problems in traditional industries, however, have proved to hinge less on labour than on management, so that as a consequence of this false diagnosis the battle has now been lost. Increasingly, competitive advantage is being assumed by countries that, a decade ago, would have been classified as Third World. The decisive factors have been design, marketing and product reliability as much as low cost. This points to high levels of management efficiency rather than to low wages as the key determining influence. The British economy may regain buoyancy and innovation, but this is unlikely to be through the regeneration of the industries into which migrants were incorporated in the immediate decades after the Second World War.

Labour market policy

If the hallmark of labour-market policy in the post-war period was an absence of official intervention, the wheel has now turned full circle. From a concentration on demand, there is now a preoccupation with both the quantity and quality of labour supply. From a period of intense labour shortage, the UK is now high in the league of industrial nations with an overall labour surplus. In an era when intervention over demand is thought to be as irrelevant as had earlier been true of supply, the issue of unemployment has assumed an unassailable position as the key political issue of the 1980s. Naturally, this has led to attempts to eradicate primary migration and threats from time to time to encourage re-migration. This last policy has never gained much ground politically in the UK, not so much because of a disinclination to act invidiously on racial grounds but because it would be overly interventionist in a strongly *laissez-faire* era.

The concentration on the quality of labour is most clearly seen in the new emphasis on training policy, which has been dubbed the 'new vocationalism'. The Conservative government has been more interventionist in this sphere than in any other, building in the process a monolithic new agency in the form of the Manpower Services Commission (MSC) and intervening in schools, which have hitherto been the preserve of local government.[1]

The result of spatial shifts in production, coupled with an unwillingness to intervene in controlling market forces, has meant that ethnic minorities have borne the brunt of the recession. For this reason it is no exaggeration to report the 'collapse' of local labour markets as far as they are concerned. The evidence for this assertion will be presented in the following section. Meanwhile training policy will be examined in more detail.

Training policy[2]

The growth of the MSC since its birth in 1973 is striking. There can be no other comparable instance in modern times of an agency of government growing in little more than a decade to a size where it threatens to outgrow its parent department of state (the Department of Education and Science). The rise of the MSC is even more striking when compared with the general pattern of public expenditure, which has been on a downward trajectory. Since 1979/80, for example, expenditure has increased threefold to £2,300 million (1985/86). This has been accompanied by an equally dramatic shift in the *pattern* of expenditure. Thus, in 1979/80, provision for school leavers under the Youth Opportunity Programme (YOP), together with temporary employment measures (usually for those a year or two older), amounted to just under one-quarter of the budget. By 1985/86, the Youth Training Scheme (YTS), which replaced YOP, alone accounted for 37 per cent of expenditure, and, when combined with the Community Programme for the long-term unemployed, the figure was nearing two-thirds of a greatly expanded budget. By 1988/89, with the coming of two-year YTS, this budget is expected to rise to £1,250 million or 47 per cent over its 1985/86 level. From an agency that was set up primarily to co-ordinate skill training provided by employers, and to facilitate the filling of vacancies, the MSC has now become a highly centralized institution for managing the labour market and for redirecting the energies of young people away from traditional job search at 16 towards further preparation for eventual employment. It has changed, therefore, from providing a service to the employed to coping with the unemployed. From helping to satisfy the demand for labour, it has become pre-occupied with perceived problems in the quality of the supply.

The New Training Initiative (NTI) of May 1981 marked a watershed in MSC policy.[3] Major training initiatives had previously lain with the Training Opportunities Scheme (TOPS) for adults and the Youth Opportunity Programme (YOP) for unemployed youngsters. However, each had experienced dramatic declines in job placement as general unemployment rose. Thus, even in the year 1980/81 itself, the proportion of white adults on TOPS courses who were in employment three months after completion of their retraining course fell from 69 per cent to 53 per cent. For ethnic minorities, the fall was similar (from 48 per cent to 36 per cent), although their employment position was worse. In fact, by the close of the year, less than one-half of whites (46 per cent) and under one-third of blacks (30 per cent) were working in the trade for which they had been trained (MSC, 1981b). Similarly, the fall in placement under YOP was as great, although not quite as dramatically sudden. In 1978, when YOP started, 68 per cent of youngsters left to enter employment; by 1981, the figure was 35 per cent (House of Commons 1983). Although the ethnic minority work-placement rate varied from region to region, it was unlikely to have exceeded 20 per cent overall by 1981.

The initial response of the MSC was to emphasize the need for a thorough-going reform of skill training on grounds that structural changes in the economy were the root cause of the problem. Thus the New Training Initiative summarized the issue in the following terms:

> The new markets and technologies require a more highly skilled, better educated and more mobile workforce in which a much larger number of professional and technical staff are supported by a range of more or less highly trained workers who perform a range of tasks and who are involved in a process rather than the repetitive assembly or manufacture of a part of a specific product. (MSC 1981a: 2)

In other words, new skills had to be taught to an upper echelon of the work force, while the others became more flexible and adaptable to technological change. On this basis the document proposed three objectives:

- To develop skill training overall.
- To provide for a comprehensive pre-vocational experience for young people.
- To extend parallel provision for adults.

Inevitably, these objectives overlap; one is concerned with *what* people know, the other two with *who* is to be trained. The important point is that, from this time onwards, the problem has been seen in largely dualistic terms. There is a perceived need to up-grade the skills of those who will lead the technological revolution and to adapt the ideas and assumptions of those remaining to a new pattern of working or non-working life.

This dualism is present in both the subsequent documents that carried the policy forward after the central ideas had been subject to public debate and governmental scrutiny (MSC 1981c; HMSO 1985). Thus the Youth Task Group Report (MSC 1982), which laid the groundwork for the current Youth Training Scheme (YTS), makes it clear that, while most of what is on offer is vocational preparation, for a minority it is intended that YTS should be the first year of vocational training analogous to the first year of an apprenticeship. The programme incorporates the previous apprenticeship support package (the Training for Skills Programme), although this only accounts for approximately 10 per cent of places. These places are with private employers, most of whom will provide their own 'off-the-job' training facilities or will have long-established relationships with further education colleges.

There are three distinct elements to the YTS. From 1984 to 1986, the first two were rather confusingly grouped together as Mode A, because they were administratively handled in a similar way. Mode B was divided (B1 and B2) into very similar parts. Overall, the *Task Group Report* made it clear that approximately two-thirds of places should be organized under the Mode A category. The dualistic element is not, as first appears, the distinction between Modes A and B; it is the removal of a small group, to be trained separately with large- or medium-sized private employers, from the remainder who then receive a pre-vocational package which at best will do little more than provide a relevant introduction to a skilled career. Thus, the distinction is between the top part of Mode A (called Mode A1 later in this chapter) and the rest.

Looking back three years later, one member of the Task Group, David Stanley (Deputy Director, Education and Training, Confederation of British Industries) clearly recognized the twin tasks that they faced:

> We all felt that there were two objectives. One was an economic objective... the preparation for work. The other was to tackle a social need because of the high level of youth unemployment. (H.C. 209 — ii 1984–85: para 102)

YTS was seen to be making a contribution to new skill needs by helping to provide a layer of technicians and skilled personnel, while at the same time providing those without qualifications with the discipline they would have previously received at work.

The attempt to counter the enforced idleness and loss of morale occasioned by the collapse in the labour market for young people was a dominant theme in one-year YTS. Gradually, there has been a move away from this reactive stance towards a more pro-active or interventionist position, in which worries over unemployment have become matched by a parallel concern for vocational training itself. This is evident in the white paper of April 1985, *Education and Training for Young People* (HMSO 1985), which, for the first time, made YTS a permanent feature of policy provision and confirmed the objective that all young people should enter the adult labour market at a minimum age of 18 with either a general educational qualification or one derived from YTS.

YTS contains, therefore, a hierarchy of provision. At its apex are schemes run by large employers using training facilities already in existence and recruiting from the pool of young people that they train. YTS under this arrangement operates like probationary employment in which a young person has a chance to prove her- or himself in a fully authentic working environment. At the other end of the scale are schemes run instead of employment, where both skill acquisition and subsequent full-time work are less likely. These schemes are often run by community organizations or charities with social rather than vocational objectives. As such, they are very worthy and often provide excellent experiences for young people. There is no doubt, however, that they are frequently regarded by scheme staff and by employers as a secondary form of training. The evidence seems to suggest that young people undergoing training of this kind will be more likely to enter the secondary sector of the labour market.

Migrants and minorities[4]
Prior to 1962, all New Commonwealth migrants were accorded rights of British citizenship under the Nationality Act 1948. In addition to legal, political and civil rights, this meant that they had a right of abode in the UK without first having to become naturalized or having to achieve a residence qualification. It follows, therefore, that these migrants are not 'foreigners' in the sense of being aliens and, of course, their children are not 'immigrants'. The fact that this label has often been retained for those of the second or even third generation is more an indication of their status as ethnic minorities than it is of their position as citizens. Moreover, the earlier a group migrated to the UK after the Second World War, the smaller the proportion of that group that has been born abroad and the more their age structure will be skewed towards the older categories. By 1983, only 2 per cent of those born in the Caribbean were under the age of 16, but 32 per cent of the more recent migrants from Bangladesh were in this category. This compares with a figure of 22 per cent for the population as a whole (OPCS 1983).

When considering the position of migrants and their descendants in relation to any facet of social or economic life in Britian, it is essential therefore to begin by recording that it is minorities and not migrant groups that must be the focus of analysis. If the problems so often associated with migration (language ability, cultural familiarity and so on) were the only ones operative in the British case, then this would not be necessary. There are relatively few

Table 3.1 Migrants* as a proportion of ethnic groups by age, 1983, per cent

Age group Years	West Indian	Indian	Ethnic group Pakistani/ Bangladeshi	All non-white†	All ethnic groups‡
0–4	–	2	8	5	1
5–9	3	10	35	18	3
10–14	4	23	37	25	3
15–19	7	50	58	32	4
20–24	26	81	92	63	6
25 and over	93	97	97	94	7
All ages	51	65	61	59	6

* Those whose stated birthplace was outside the UK.
† Including some groups not shown in this table.
‡Including those whose ethnic origin was not stated.
Source: HMSO (1983)

young migrants in the UK, and their difficulties almost certainly parallel those that have been recorded elsewhere. Those who are of migrant origin however, and who are still identifiable by racial or cultural characteristics, are a much larger proportion of the total. The extent to which this is true can be seen from Table 3.1, which compares the number of actual migrants with the total size of the minority community in three cases. It demonstrates that, in 1983, 93 per cent of those in the 15- to 19-year-old category who could claim West Indian ethnicity or racial origin were in fact British born. The proportion declines for those from minority communities that have become more recently established. For example, in the 10- to 14-year age band, more than one-third of those claiming Pakistani or Bangladeshi origins were in fact born abroad. Thus, whatever hypotheses may be formulated on the assumption that migratory processes themselves have an effect on, say, school performance or training success, they will only have relevance for a proportion of those who are migrant descended – often a small and declining proportion. For this reason, this chapter refers to the migrants and their descendants in British society as 'ethnic minorities'. This is not to say that migration itself is unimportant, nor that the minorities identified here are the only ones that could be separately considered. The relatively early experience of post-war labour migration, together with the citizenship rights accorded to

Table 3.2 Proportion of West Indians and Asians living in conurbations, England and Wales, per cent

Ethnic group	1961	1966	1971	1983*
West Indian	79.5	78.4	76.7	80
Asian	56.0	59.2	61.5	70
Total population	40.7	38.7	36.6	29

* Metropolitan counties from HMSO (1983)
Source: Field *et al.* (1981).

those from the old British Empire, as well as the continuing significance of race and ethnicity in the distribution of life chances and opportunities, makes it irrelevant to speak of migrants in the same way that is common in the rest of Europe. At the same time, it is necessary to designate a separate and identifiable category for those of migrant origin.

When it comes to the term 'second generation', a difficult terrain is entered. For a start, it is inaccurate. Young people entering the labour market in 1987/88 may have been born in 1970. Their parents could have been born in 1950 or even later. Thus, in the British case, ethnic minorities are entering their third generation. More importantly, however, the term carries with it a connotation of 'foreignness', as if the origins of one's parents had a necessary effect on current status. This is clearly true in some other European countries, but not in the UK. The term will only be used, therefore, to effect comparisons with other European minorities.

The size and distribution of the minority population
The age structure of the original migrant population, together with the subsequent processes of family completion and higher levels of age-specific fertility, have assured a rapid growth in the minority population. The latest estimates suggest a growth of the West Indian, Asian and other New Commonwealth population from 673,497, or 1.5 per cent of the total population, in 1961 to 1,771,000, or 3.3 per cent, in 1976. The national census does not contain a question on race or ethnicity, so that it is, in this regard, of lesser value than sample surveys. Those born in the New Commonwealth and Pakistan rose from 2.12 per cent of the population in 1971 to 2.38

per cent in 1981; this is a net increase of approximately 400,000. However, the census does permit the calculation of numbers of people living in a household headed by someone born in the New Commonwealth or Pakistan. In 1981, this figure came to 2.2 million people or almost 4.1 per cent of Britain's household population in that year. Sample surveys, although less reliable, are often more up to date. The Labour Force Survey of 1983, for example, shows that for the UK 0.92 per cent recorded their ethnicity as 'West Indian or Guyanese', 1.45 per cent as 'Indian', 0.65 per cent as 'Pakistani' and 0.15 per cent as 'Bangladeshi', making a total of 3.17 per cent from these major ethnic groupings. By 1985, the total ethnic minority population is given from the same source as 2.4 million, or 4.4 per cent of the total. Of these, just over half a million either came or are descended from those who arrived from the Caribbean, while a million are 'Asian' in origin (including one-sixth from East Africa). A significant proportion of the remainder are given as 'mixed' in ethnic origin (Department of Employment 1987b).

The censuses reveal that this ethnic minority population has been predominantly urban in its location. Table 3.2 shows the small amount of change there has been over the last two decades in the proportions of either main ethnic category who have moved outside the urban areas into the suburbs, small towns or beyond. Although there have been some dramatic alterations in the distribution of minorities within the conurbations, it is still true to say that these populations are heavily concentrated in urban areas. More precisely, there are two other reasons for such concentrations. Firstly, it is not all conurbations that contain significant proportions of minority populations. Largely as a result of economic opportunities in the 1950s and 1960s, the West-Indian and Asian-descended population is now heavily concentrated in the Greater London area and the West and East Midlands. For example, the 1985 Labour Force Survey showed that 72 per cent of those of Caribbean origin who are economically active live in Greater London and the West Midlands (Department of Employment 1987b). Similarly, 62 per cent of economically active 'Indians' and 45 per cent of 'Pakistanis and Bangladeshis' live in the same two locations.

The second reason for such population concentrations is the extent to which Asian and West Indian minorities are found in the central areas of British cities. Partly as a result of housing opportunities after arrival, and partly as a product of subsequent shifts in the white population, there has been a progressive tendency for Asians in particular to be increasingly concentrated in certain parts of the inner cities. Limitations on access to publicly provided housing, together with discrimination and an inability to purchase more expensive housing in the suburbs, forced both groups to rent private accommodation that was usually in the poorest and oldest parts of the inner areas. Evidence suggests that the concentration of ethnic minorities in the core areas of Britain's major cities is increasing. For example, in the London metropolitan region, there was a rise of 2.3 per cent in the population born in the New Commonwealth between 1971 and 1981, compared with an overall rise of half this amount. Similar comparisons between 'core' and 'peripheral' areas in other cities suggest the same process is occurring elsewhere. The reason is not so much that of movement by minorities themselves but is owing to selective outward movement by whites. This is a process that is now so marked that it is becoming common to find wards, or smaller areas of cities, which have more than a half of their populations living in the households headed by someone of New Commonwealth migrant origin.

The age structure of minority populations
In the 1983 Labour Force Survey, those who had classified themselves of West Indian, Pakistani or Bangladeshi origin, or who were born in these countries, accounted for 3 per cent of the total population of the UK. What is of interest, however, is that the proportion from these communities is larger in the younger age groups, so that 6 per cent of the 0- to 4-year-old group came from these origins, and 5 per cent in those from 5 to 9 years of age. As would be expected, the representation of minorities is higher, therefore, in younger age groups. In the 1985 survey, this pattern is confirmed; ethnic minorities accounted for 7.3 per cent of the population under 16, but only 0.7 per cent of those in their retirement years (Department of Employment 1987b.) A corollary of this is that 70 per cent of Afro-Caribbeans and of East African Asians are of working age, although the greater tendency for other Asian minorities to be young means that these other Asian minorities approximate to the white population in terms of the proportion who can be part of the labour market. For example, almost half those of Pakistani and Bangladeshi origin are under 16 years old, indicating a considerable growth potential over the next two decades.

Labour market incorporation
The ethnic minority population of the UK has, in the past, revealed high levels of economic activity, mainly because that was the reason for original migration. This differs from some other European minorities, where the main purpose was education or vocational training. Moreover, when compared with the adult population as a whole, economic activity rates have been high because there are

so few members of ethnic minority groups who are in retirement. The Labour Force Survey of 1985 shows that, when comparisons are made with those of working years (16–64 for males; 16–59 for females), a smaller proportion of minority men and women are economically active (80 to 88 per cent for men; 52 to 67 per cent for women). This is largely accounted for by the far greater likelihood that ethnic minorities will stay on at school or further education and also by the fact that Asian women (particularly Pakistani/ Bangladeshi) are less likely than others to be in the labour market. These two phenomena can be clearly seen in Figures 3.1 and 3.2. What is equally clear is that 'West Indian' women in their later years are particularly active, having participation rates at least as high, and often higher, than others.

In terms of location within the industrial structure, the position is relatively clear. All ethnic groups are over-represented in those industries to which they were originally recruited. Thus, men of Caribbean origin are strongly over-represented in engineering and transport, while women predominate in service industries. Asians are concentrated in manufacturing and distribution (Department of Employment 1982). What is perhaps more important is that original patterns of incorporation at the lowest levels also have not changed to any marked degree. With the exception of those of Indian descent, who include significant proportions of medically qualified men, ethnic minorities still tend to be concentrated at the bottom of the socio-economic distributions. Thus, the 1981 survey data reveal that only 13 per cent of employed West Indian men are in non-manual jobs compared with 40 per cent of the employed white male population. For women, the pattern is similar but less extreme (ibid.: 22). A high proportion of the West Indian non-manual employees are probably located in the lower echelons of the nursing profession or in clerical work. It is certainly not clear that the apparently greater degree of integration of women has, in fact, been achieved. Just as minority men tend to be concentrated in the least skilled manual jobs or in the less desirable skilled areas, so, too, are minority women probably found in the least attractive sectors of non-manual employment.

This general conclusion is also supported by other survey data, which show that, while educational attainment does improve job prospects, ethnic-minority employees with lower levels of educational attainment are far more likely than whites to be excluded from non-manual employment (Brown 1984: 199). In fact ethnic minorities overall are at least as likely as whites to possess 'higher' level qualifications. This is particularly true of men, but there is an important difference between ethnic groups. Thus Afro-Caribbeans

67

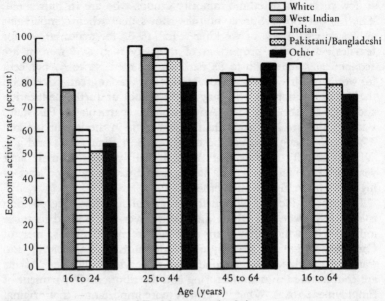

Source: Department of Employment (1987)

Figure 3.1a Economic activity rates by ethnic origin and age: males, Great Britain Spring 1985

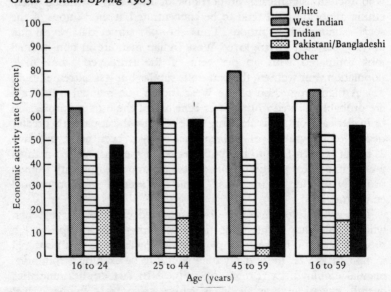

Source: Department of Employment (1987)

Figure 3.1b Economic activity rates by ethnic origin and age: females, Great Britain Spring 1985

and Pakistanis/Bangladeshis are less likely to have 'higher' qualifications than whites, whereas Indians and those of 'mixed' origins are more likely to (Department of Education, 1987a: 24). These differentials are most marked amongst the young and are more true for men than women. Lower socio-economic levels are not simply a function of industrial distributions. That is, regardless of the industrial sector, ethnic-minority employees are likely to be over-represented at the lower levels (Brown 1984: 207).

Of course, socio-economic group is a poor indicator of an individual's command over resources. The evidence in this area is far from complete, but what there is tends to suggest that minorities are likely to earn less than their white peers, the higher the socio-economic level they achieve. For example, Field et al. (1981) have suggested that minority males in professional employment achieved only 75 per cent of the income gained by white professionals. This compares with over 100 per cent of the income earned by semi-skilled and unskilled manual workers. The reasons for this latter 'success' may be associated with the age structure of the minority population, the greater prevalence of shift work and the tendency for minorities to work longer hours than whites. The same authors conclude:

> Owing to a combination of low earnings, a high proportion of dependants and higher housing costs, it is likely that minority households experience a greater degree of poverty than do white households: (Field et al. 1981: 34)

Other evidence is less clear-cut and tends to show that income differences are similar, regardless of socio-economic level, whether shifts are worked or age level (Brown 1984: 214).

As far as young people are concerned, the evidence is not entirely conclusive. The data obtained from the National Dwelling and Housing Survey suggest that the same picture holds as for adults, except that the minority population approximates more closely that of the majority. For example, nearly 60 per cent of West Indian males are given as falling in the 'skilled manual' category, compared with only 42 per cent for the white population.

The relationship between socio-economic status, industrial location and income is complex. As far as net income is concerned the relative position of ethnic minorities may, for example, become worse at higher income levels (Field et al. 1981). This is borne out for ethnic-minority men by a recent survey (Table 3.3), but not for women who, by contrast, are shown as receiving a higher income than whites at all socio-economic levels. These data must be accepted with great caution, since small numbers are involved, and they merge Asians with West Indians (Brown 1984).

Table 3.3   *Asian and West Indian median weekly earnings as a percentage of white earnings by socio-economic group, 1981, full-time employees*

	Males	Females
Professional, employer, manager	82	114
Other non-manual	96	105
Skilled manual and foreman	92	111
Semi-skilled manual	91 ⎫	109
Unskilled manual	98 ⎭	
All	85	101

Source: adapted from Brown (1984).

Table 3.4   *Net personal income for employed inner city residents by race and gender, 1981 per cent*

Net weekly income £	Male White	Asian	West Indian	Female White	Asian	West Indian
Under 10	2	2	1	43	45	30
40–59	11	13	25	28	33	44
60–79	31	40	42	17	12	19
80–99	25	23	20	9	5	4
100–149	26	20	10	3	5	0
150 upward	5	2	1	0	0	3
Total	100	100	100	100	100	100
(N)	(171)	(258)	(79)	(137)	(82)	(103)

Source: Cross and Johnson (forthcoming).

The data in Table 3.4 come from a household survey carried out in 1981 (Cross and Johnson forthcoming) and are perhaps more satisfactory. Instead of supplying media income data, they are based on a range and they control for locality, being derived solely from inner-city locations in the West Midlands. It is clear that West Indian men do indeed gather the poorest returns from their employment. Fewer than one-third received a net personal income of more than £80 per week, compared with 56 per cent of white males. West Indian women, by contrast, fared slightly better, but the data are not controlled for hours worked, and West Indian women are known to work longer hours than others.

Unemployment and the inner city economy
Throughout Europe, the majority of the 15 million migrant labourers can be found concentrated in the inner areas of the older industrial cities in which they first settled. The only exceptions are where, as in some mining areas, the original employment was not in an urban industry and where the distribution of migrant labour was centrally controlled (for example West Germany). The twin processes of class concentration and of racial exclusion have ensured that ethnic minorities are now totally dependent upon the fortunes of inner-city economies. The former was the reason for the original settlement patterns, but these have become firmly entrenched by racism. In the British case, ethnic-minority communities owe much of their internal cohesion to these processes rather than to similarity of culture. What identity of cultural expression exists is at least as much the product of a similarity of structural position, allied to a common experience of racist exclusion, as it is to the pre-existence of an Afro-Caribbean or Asian cultural form.

Inner-city economies have not remained static since the 1950s and 1960s. By the mid-1970s, there were signs of a massive new transformation. The two most important features of these changes were, firstly, the rapid decline of industries that had been the mainstays of the urban economy and, secondly, the relocation of other more buoyant companies to the suburbs, small towns or overseas. International competition in manufacturing coupled with the recessionary impact of a downswing in the trade-cycle and, above all, the growth of new technology have created a new social geography of production (Massey 1984). Part of this has been to exacerbate a long-established trend for economic resources to shift to the south of England but, more importantly for ethnic minorities, it has been accompanied by an unprecedented decline in inner-city economies, the most significant indicator of which is the level of unemployment in these areas.

A central feature of the early period of migration to the UK was the low level of unemployment. This was because employment prospects were the prime motive for migration (Peach 1968). Since that early period, however, the picture has altered dramatically, and what was once an almost complete incorporation of West Indians and Asian into employment has now become a much more tenuous

Table 3.5   Unemployment rates by age, sex and ethnic origin, 1985

| Ethnic origin | Unemployment rate* | | | |
| | 16 to 24 years | | All of working age | |
	Men	Women	Men	Women
White	18	15	11	10
Afro-Caribbean	32	34	23	19
Indian	28	20	18	15
Pakistani/Bangladeshi	37	–	28	44
Other	28	38	17	18
All	18	15	11	10

* Per cent unemployed of those economically active
Source: Department of Employment (1987b), table 9.

and fragile relationship. As Table 3.5 shows, young people generally are about 50 per cent more likely to be unemployed than is true overall. Afro-Caribbean and Pakistani/Bangladeshi men and women are particularly likely to be unemployed. It is very important to note that, although educational qualifications are an asset, they do not account for the differentials in Table 3.5. Thus the same survey shows that for white males (16 to 64 years) the chances of unemployment dropped from 17 per cent for those with no qualifications to 3 per cent when they had higher qualifications. For ethnic minorities, the fall is less dramatic, from 26 per cent to 11 per cent. This can be seen by standardizing ethnic-minority rates on white rates so that 100 is equal to the same proportion out of work. The figures then are:

	Men	Women
Higher qualifications	333	100
Other qualifications	233	220
No qualifications	153	167

Thus only women with 'higher qualifications' have the same unemployment rate as white women. This position seems to have declined relative to whites since the early 1980s.

The reasons for this problem are both simple and complex. At a simple level, it is just a shortage of jobs at skill levels appropriate to inner-city populations. At a more complex and subtle level, there is clearly a major association between inner-city decline, particularly in areas where manufacturing and engineering jobs have been lost, and differential chances of unemployment. There is a strong correlation, for example, between minority concentration, unemployment and city change through internal migration (Cross 1986b). For example, Hackney, Islington and Lambeth are the London boroughs with the highest proportions of households headed by someone of Caribbean origin. They also rank second, third and fourth in terms of unemployment (after Tower Hamlets). Over the inter-censual period 1971–1981, each of these boroughs lost about one-fifth of their population as so-called 'white flight' gathered momentum. In the West Midlands, the story is the same: Wolverhampton has the highest proportion of ethnic minorities in the area, the highest unemployment rate and ranks fourth in population loss. Birmingham has a slightly smaller proportion of black citizens, a marginally lower unemployment rate and the highest level of population loss in the West Midlands. At a local level, the association between minority concentration and unemployment is even more compelling. In Handsworth, Birmingham, for example, which was the scene of widespread urban unrest in September 1985, the rate of adult male unemployment is 44 per cent (August 1986), and seven out of ten households are headed by someone born in Asia or the Caribbean. Unemployment is high for everyone in the inner city but this situation affects West Indians and Asians more because that is where the vast majority are located. The study by Brown, for example, shows that male West Indians in inner London, inner Birmingham and inner Manchester had an unemployment rate of 29 per cent, compared with 23 per cent for whites. The central point here is not so much 'race' but 'space', since 41 per cent of blacks lived in these areas, compared with only 6 per cent of whites (Brown 1984: 192). Thus the experience of unemployment for different groups is partly a function of location and industry. Age, too, makes a difference for a similar reason: unemployment amongst the young is higher is general, and higher proportions of blacks than of whites fall into vulnerable age bands.

Occupational aspirations
There is an impressive literature on the so-called 'transition from school work'. However, although discussion frequently takes place on the significance of occupational aspirations, educational qualifications and job-search practices, there is frequently an underlying assumption that this transition is a smooth process unaffected by wider structural constraints. There is evidence to suggest that minority youngsters are particularly keen to pursue skilled or white-collar work. A slight difference exists between Afro-Caribbean young people, who favour skilled employment and trades,

73

Table 3.6 *Occupational aspirations of Asian and Afro-Caribbean young people when compared with whites at the age of 16, 1986, per cent*

Occupational group	Asians	Whites	Afro-Caribbeans	Whites
Managerial/ professional technical	16	9	14	6
Clerical	34	30	29	35
Skilled manual	40	46	49	42
Semi-skilled/ unskilled	3	11	2	13
Unknown	6	4	5	3
Total	100	100	100	100

Source: adapted from Cross, Wrench and Barnet (1987).

and Asians, who are more likely to opt for becoming technicians, laboratory assistants or other technical staff (Cross and Wrench 1987). The latest evidence is given in Table 3.6, which is derived from a study of young people passing through the careers counselling service (Cross, Wrench and Barnet, 1987). In it, the young people are matched by educational attainment, so that the comparisons are between Asian young people and equivalently qualified whites, and Afro-Caribbeans and a second control group of whites. Much of what is often taken as the 'unrealistic' aspirations of Asians in particular is accounted for by the tendency of these young people to perform well at school. What Table 3.6 demonstrates is that, when this ambition is taken into account, there is still a slight tendency for ethnic minorities to aim a little higher in the occupational spectrum. The reasons for this are probably associated with the pressure from parents for their offspring to achieve what they may not have managed. It is, of course, well known that migrants or their immediate descendants are likely to seek occupational improvements to justify and vindicate their original decision to tear up their roots and make an uncomfortable transition to an inhospitable industrial setting.

Inevitably, intentions are themselves highly changeable, since they are dependent upon individual judgments of the opportunity structure. It would come as no surprise, for example, to discover

Table 3.7   Vocational aspirations of minority young people

	West Indian		Asian		Indigenous	
	Male	Female	Male	Female	Male	Female
Apprenticeships	43	1	52	2	31	2
Clerical	0	7	1	5	1	5
Other skilled	3	4	14	11	14	4
Semi-skilled/ unskilled	5	2	6	9	7	4
Stay at school	35	69	14	38	18	43
Further education	2	8	6	26	8	18
No information	11	9	6	9	19	21
Total	100	100	100	100	100	100
(N)	(161)	(90)	(98)	(85)	(220)	(144)

Source: adapted from Lee and Wrench (1981).

that, as openings for young people decline generally, a higher proportion of those about to reach the minimum school-leaving age decide to stay on and obtain further qualifications. Some interesting data on this process is contained in Table 3.7, which is derived from a survey conducted in the West Midlands. The data suggest two obvious conclusions which have been largely substantiated by other research. The first implication is that, as far as minority status is concerned, young males are particularly keen to enter the most rigorous form of vocational training for skilled employment. Afro-Caribbean boys, in particular, seem to be enthusiastic to pursue apprenticeships. The second implication is that vocational aspirations at this stage of development caused young women to opt for an alternative strategy. In general, this is to stay on at school or in further education for as long as possible, although there is evidence of a difference between the sub-groups. It appears, for example, as if young Asian girls are more prepared to pursue academic qualifications than Afro-Caribbeans and whites, who seem more interested in further education containing a much higher proportion of vocational training. There is certainly no suggestion, however, that young members of minority groups are uninterested in training opportunities or in aspiring to skilled employment.

It is sometimes claimed that minority young people reveal 'unrealistic' aspirations in that their wishes are unlikely to be reached either because of a shortage of skilled jobs or because of their own low level of achievement. Certainly, this is the view of careers officers and others concerned with the advice and placement of young people in school or further education (Careers Bulletin 1978: 24). It is hard to find evidence from the research literature itself, however, to support this conclusion (Fowler *et al.* 1977). A study of West Indian males, for example, which compared their occupational aspirations with a group of white boys matched for educational performance, shows that in only 14.2 per cent of cases did the West Indians aspire to non-manual employment compared with nearly 26 per cent of the matched whites (Dex 1981). In direct conflict with this, however, the same study then shows that assessments by youth employment officers suggested that only three out of five Afro-Caribbeans were 'fully suitable' for their desired jobs compared with three-quarters of the white group. The study concludes that the reasons for this disparity lie more with the perceptions of the professional staff than they do with the underlying aspirations of the young people themselves.

An additional issue of importance concerns the attempts made by young people to obtain the jobs they desire. Both a consideration of the applications they make, and the methods by which they seek out information on job vacancies, are needed. In relation to the former, there is evidence — although unavailable by age group — that the unemployed differ in the number of formal applications they made in the month prior to interview and that race is an important predictor of these differences (Smith 1981). In this research, Afro-Caribbeans are shown to lead the field, with men making on average 4.4 applications in the previous month and women 4.3. White men, by contrast, made 3.7 applications and white women 2.4 on average. Indian applicants showed slightly less signs of having gone through the formal channels, and Smith concludes that this is probably because they are more active on an informal front. As far as young people are concerned, a study, by the Commission for Racial Equity, in Lewisham (South London) shows that blacks tried just as hard as whites to find employment but with substantially less success (CRE 1978). Although this latter study does reveal that the black applicants had fewer qualifications, the lack of success that occurred was not entirely attributable to these differences. Smith (1981) indicates that all of those unemployed are likely to use the official agencies of job placement more than any other avenue. When it comes to young people, West Indian males are particularly likely to use the careers service as the major part of their job search. The same is, on the whole, true for young women, although for Asians of both sexes are less likely to employ these official agencies.

It appears that those with less capacity to communicate in English are more likely to employ unofficial means of job attainment. Informal job-search methods tend to produce lower levels of occupational position, since family contacts tend not to be able to provide access to skilled employment unless the family already possesses members in higher-level employment (Dex 1981: 33). As young people grow older their reliance upon formal channels of job placement declines, although a study of Afro-Caribbeans suggests that they avoid using methods of job location that will expose them to greater risks of discrimination. More than half of a sample of young Afro-Caribbean males avoided a direct approach to an employer, while 40 per cent similarly eschewed contacts by telephone (Sillitoe 1980: 15). There are considerable differences between the sexes, although the overwhelming conclusion must remain that minority young people are more likely than whites to employ official agencies to secure their first job.

Access to MSC provision
The provision of places under the Youth Opportunities Programme (YOP) expanded rapidly from its inception in 1978 until it was phased out in 1983. In 1979–80, some 216,000 entrants were recorded, the vast majority of them experiencing both a short-training course of work preparation and a subsequent period of work experience on an employer's premises. By 1982, the throughput had risen to 553,000, comprising about one in two minimum-age school-leavers. Ethnic minority young people were fully represented on these courses, even allowing for the fact that they were intended for the unemployed, who contained a disproportionate number of black youngsters (Cross *et al.* 1983). However, the YOP provided very little by way of vocational training as such but was much more concerned with preparatory courses, including remedial education and so-called 'social and life skills'. Moreover, ethnic minority young people were more likely to find themselves in preparatory and remedial courses and much less so to be introduced to work in a large high technology company (ibid.). As a result, they were also less likely to translate their experiences under YOP into subsequent employment.

The important question that arises is the extent to which minorities have permeated the Youth Training Scheme (YTS), which commenced in September 1983. Official MSC statistics suggest that ethnic minorities of Afro-Caribbean or Asian origin accounted for about 3.5 per cent of YTS recruits or starters. This is a surprisingly low figure, for youthful populations experiencing a disproportionate incidence of unemployment. Ethnic-minority youngsters are less evident on Mode A YTS, where the 'managing agency' is contracted to an employer or private training organization. Further light is thrown on this important point in Figure 3.3. Seven out of ten white young men on YTS can expect to get on to a Mode A scheme and more than four out of five white girls. Fewer than half the Afro-Caribbean boys, however, are recruited to Mode A, the majority being sent on community projects, into training workshops or similar schemes. The under-representation of other groups on Mode A is similar but less extreme. Ethnic-minority youngsters are therefore less likely to enter companies that will offer them a subsequent chance of specialization and skilled employment.

The *Task Group Report* establishing YTS not only drew a distinction between Mode A and Mode B but also within each mode of funding (MSC 1982). Most of YTS is pre-vocational or non-vocational, but it also varies according to whether or not it is oriented towards employment in industry or towards community work. Research on YTS has tended to show, unsurprisingly, that Mode A1, with its chance of starting on a skilled career in industry, is greatly preferred to other Modes or schemes (Fenton *et al.* 1984). Unfortunately the ethnic statistics produced by the MSC do not permit a ready classification into Mode A1 and Mode A2. This can be worked out locally by reclassifying individual schemes. The data for the Birmingham and Solihull area show, for example, that nearly one in three white young people in 1983–85 on YTS were on a scheme run by a private company. This was true for only one in eight young people of Afro-Caribbean or Asian origin (Cross 1986a).

Mode A1 is, of course, far from homogeneous. It includes a very high proportion of places organized by the Large Companies Unit of the MSC, and employers are drawn from both the secondary and tertiary sectors. An attempt is made to incorporate this division in Figure 3.2, which shows the dramatic under-representation of ethnic-minority youngsters in the private employer sections of Mode A1. These data are expressed by comparing the representation of Afro-Caribbean and Asian youngsters against whites and expressing the figure as an index. Parity of representation is achieved when the index is zero, because this means that the proportion of ethnic minorities on this type of scheme is equal to the proportion of whites on the same scheme (Cross 1986a). What can be readily perceived is that on Mode A1, ethnic minorities are under-represented. Moving further away from the chances of real vocational training increases the representation of minorities, so that, for every 100 white youngsters on Mode B2, there are more than 300 from ethnic-minority origins. This disparity cannot be accounted for by

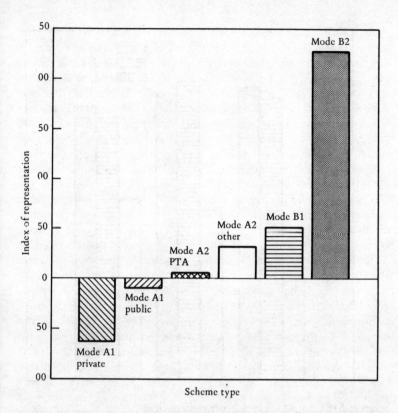

Source: Birmingham and Solihull Area Manpower Board (1984–85). (Unpublished statistics).

Figure 3.2 Index of representation of ethnic minorities by mode, Birmingham 1985

differences in the accessibility of schemes or by the educational quali-fications of scheme applicants (Cross and Smith 1987).

MSC follow-up data gathered in 1985 shows what happens to young people after they leave YTS. Overall, Mode A schemes have the highest success rate in helping youngsters to obtain jobs. As Figure 3.3 shows, whites who have been on Mode A schemes are much less likely to be unemployed six months after leaving than are Afro-Caribbeans or Asians. Unfortunately all young people who have been on Modes B1/B2 are as likely to be unemployed as in work after leaving. Thus, ethnic minorities face two problems: they are less likely to get on the better schemes and, once there, they are less likely to translate that experience into subsequent

79

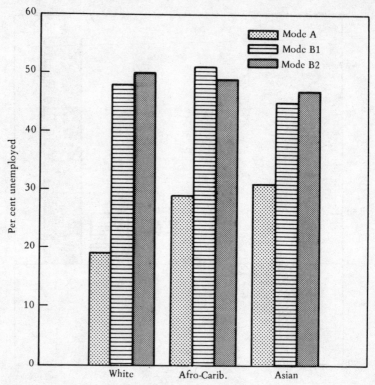

Source: MSC (1985) (Unpublished statistics)

Figure 3.3 Probability of entering unemployment after YTS by mode and race

employment. This last point can be seen from Figure 3.4, which shows how important the low level of representation on the better parts of Mode A is for subsequent employment prospects of ethnic minorities (Cross 1986a).

Training assumptions
The MSC has consistently assumed that black minorities in British society have 'special needs'. In the early period when YOP for the 'least able' and least employable was developed, the whole administration was subsumed under a 'special programmes' division. This division commissioned five reports under the rubric 'Special programmes: special needs', one of which was on ethnic-minority young people (MSC 1979). This document, which was prepared

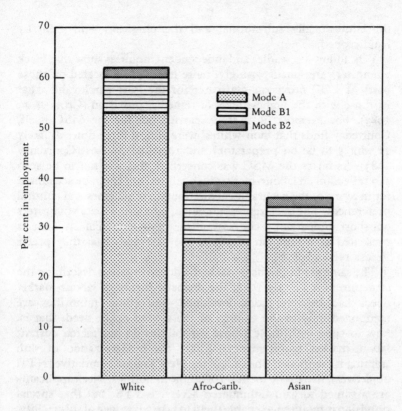

Source: MSC Scheme Occupancy Statistics (1985–86) and follow-up survey (1985). (Unpublished statistics)

Figure 3.4 Maximum proportion of YTS leavers in employment by mode and race

in collaboration with the Commission for Racial Equality, recounted the evidence on discrimination and argued a case for targeted vocational training (under sections 35 and 37 of the Race Relations Act 1976). It also recommended more consultation with minority communities and greater efforts at attracting young blacks on to training programmes. The report's findings were rejected. The overriding view prevailed that ethnic minorities were more in need of remedial provision and 'preparatory courses', which were designed to overcome their putative deficiencies in employability. The bracketing of black youngsters with the other 'problem' groups makes this clear. 'Special needs' were also felt to exist for young offenders, the educationally sub-normal and the physically and mentally handicapped.

YOP follow-up studies and independent inquiries show that black youngsters are, unsurprisingly, more likely to be located on those parts of YOP provision that cater for the least employable, that is, those with the highest level of remedial provision (Cross *et al.* 1983). For example, in a study carried out for the MSC itself, Courtenay finds that 'non-whites' were almost three times as likely as whites to be on preparatory and remedial courses (Courtenay 1983). As far as the MSC was concerned, this was not to be seen as a reflection on labour-market inequalities, but could be accounted for in terms of the geographical distribution of schemes and cultural preferences. The over-representation of ethnic-minority youngsters on short preparatory courses or on basic remedial training is presented as a function of where they are and what they prefer (Cross 1986a, 1987b).

The same assumptions pervade the documentation describing the structure of YTS. By 1982, the dualistic theory of labour-market needs had become more developed, and ethnic minorities are mentioned only in the context of the second major need: that is, how to cope with those whose capabilities do not match current labour-market requirements. Where the modernization of skill training is mentioned (the first of the New Training Initiative [NTI] objectives), there is no mention of ethnic minorities. Black applicants are assumed to gain unhindered access to YTS, but that special provision is required to enable them to take advantage of this facility. In 1982, following the reorganization of MSC and the reintegration of training under a new training division, one section was specifically charged with 'policy on work preparation, race relations and industrial language training'. The annual report for that year makes it abundantly clear that ethnic minorities are particularly in need of preparatory courses (MSC 1982b). For example, these courses are only discussed in a section entitled 'ethnic minorities' and are therefore not perceived as suitable for others. The Commission's policy is described as one of 'concentrating special training provision (for example preparatory courses) in those areas where disadvantaged groups predominate' (MSC 1982b: 34). As far as adults are concerned, preparatory courses are again mentioned as specifically suitable for blacks, as are literacy and numeracy training and the provision of language training courses (MSC 1982b: 34). Furthermore, in the later discussion paper on adult training (MSC 1983) in pursuit of the third NTI objective, ethnic minorities are only included in the second task of 'non-vocational' training for the unemployed. Thus:

> Basic (non-occupational) education and training opportunities must be preserved and improved for those who have been out of employment for some time or who, like the disabled, ethnic minorities and women returning to work, may suffer disadvantage which can be remedied by training, in getting a job. (MSC 1983a: 11)

The black unemployed are therefore perceived as suffering a 'disadvantage', which can be remedied by 'non-occupational' training.

There is little doubt, therefore, as to what the 'needs' of ethnic minorities are seen as being. They are regarded as 'disadvantaged' in the labour market and therefore particularly suited to pre-training interventions designed to enhance employability. With the coming of the two-year YTS in April 1986, there appeared, at first sight, to be a move away from this position. The new proposals followed from a significant shift in government policy towards greater emphasis on skill training itself and away from merely a containment strategy on unemployment. Moreover, the White Paper announcing these developments emphasizes the need for 'employers to make a substantial contribution towards the costs of the new scheme' (HMSO 1985: 8). The old Mode A/Mode B distinction has been abandoned, and schemes can now be run only by designated Approved Training Organizations (ATOs). The MSC itself has responded to criticisms of the previous arrangements by confirming:

> It will be essential to eradicate the false perception of first and second class trainees within the scheme which is closely identified with the existing mode structure. (MSC 1985: 9)

Under the new policy, the funding procedure is for an ATO to receive £110 per contracted place per year, plus £160 for each filled place per month.

Despite this apparently signifcant shift in emphasis and design, the underlying pattern of the new scheme is very similar. The system is entirely voluntary on the part of employers, and, since only one in five companies participate at all, this means that places cannot be guaranteed. There must be a subsidiary arrangement to provide places where a shortfall exists or for those young people who are not wanted by employers and training organizations. Under the new arrangements, the residual Mode B schemes are run by ATOs, who receive an additional payment of £110 per place filled. Because of this extra payment, these places are known as 'premium' places. The Under Secretary of State for Employment has summarized the reasons for the introduction of premium places in these terms:

> Premium places have been introduced in recognition of the extra costs faced by providers of training programmes for young people with special

training needs and to ensure provision in areas where sufficient employer based places may not be available. (House of Commons 1986)

Those who are regarded as 'disadvantaged', and who live in areas of high unemployment, cannot expect a place with an employer. Rather, they will occupy a place in a new secondary sector, which is more focused than before on catering for 'special needs'. Many are concerned that the difficulties of the previous scheme, whereby ethnic-minority young people were particularly likely to have their actual training needs unmet, will be continued. The implication is that current inequalities in the labour market will be replicated for the new generation.

Labour market mobility

Occupational mobility within one generation will first be discussed and then some brief observations on inter-generational change will be made. If it is assumed that skills gained from a prior occupation are still relevant to employment in the UK, there should be a reasonable correlation between the level of jobs held in Asia and the West Indies and that currently held in the UK. The survey in the West Midlands (Cross and Johnson forthcoming) reported on earlier shows that, for male Afro-Caribbean migrants, the effect of migration itself is largely negative. Female migrants generally appear to have gained more from their relocation. For males, while over half of those previously in 'craft or skilled' occupations were still in such jobs (and a relatively low number unemployed), very few had achieved higher-graded jobs and a substantial number (over one-quarter) were in less skilled posts. Non-manual workers were overwhelmingly concentrated in engineering and manual jobs, and one-quarter were unemployed. Farmers who had owned their own land were generally worse off in employment terms (and particularly in unemployment) than those who had been wage labourers, who were now less likely to be in assembly-line positions. Few wage labourers, in particular, had penetrated the higher-rank jobs in skilled or non-manual positions. For women, there was an appreciable penetration of intermediate and 'non-manual' (or non-industrial) positions by former wage labourers and artisans, although the former had an unenviable unemployment record. Amongst those who had entered the labour market only after migration, males were particularly affected by unemployment and, while a substantial proportion of males were now in skilled engineering trades, none had obtained 'non-manual' jobs. For females, the situation was rather more favourable (Cross and Johnson forthcoming).

The same study shows that the period during which migration

took place has had some effect on mobility chances. A fairly crude analysis of the time of migration by present occupation shows how earlier migrants are somewhat more likely to have moved into higher-order jobs, but that, in general, there is remarkable consistency among the proportions of males in skilled occupations and females in service industries. Later, female migrants are more likely to have found office employment, while earlier male migrants are still concentrated in transport and manual positions. Only the most recent male migrants were in professional, managerial or intermediate occupations to any significant extent, suggesting a qualitatively different kind of migration.

The second aspect of intra-generational change concerns the career developments of migrants after migration. For this, data is needed on first occupations after migration and on current occupation. The Policy Studies Institute (PSI) survey of 1982 provides some understanding of this phenomenon, although unfortunately the data are for combined West Indian and Asian respondents, and they refer to a fixed-time comparison rather than to first jobs after migration. This study shows a small amount of intra-generational change affecting 7 per cent of men and women. Of this, there was a net upward change affecting only 3 per cent of men and 1 per cent of women, so there is little reason to think that many barriers to career enhancement have been removed (Brown 1984: 227).

Intra-generational mobility is, of course, a continuing process, and each change of job provides an opportunity for social improvement or a loss of status. The West Midlands survey was not able to record full work histories, but, for those who had been in their current job for less than ten years, there was evidence on the job from which they had moved. For Afro-Caribbean males, the most recent job change had led to a lower-ranking position more often than the opposite, while only half as many whites had lost by their move. Afro-Caribbean females, again, showed greater upward mobility, although closer examination of the data reveals that this derives from a move out of unskilled or semi-skilled factory employment (assembly-line work) into manual service work (cleaning and hairdressing), from which the benefits are likely to be slight.

As far as inter-generational mobility is concerned, there are major problems in arriving at an unambiguous data set. This is mainly a function of attempting to compare a group in one labour market with those in another, when the markets themselves are so different. For example, Asian migrants often came from rural backgrounds and always moved from a predominantly rural economy. What can be concluded, therefore, when they end up in jobs that are not agricultural? The best solution is to confine attention to that minority that did not come from farming or subsistence agriculture. Cross and Johnson (forthcoming) show that, when this is done, upward movement is far more likely for whites than for Asians and Afro-Caribbeans in the same areas of British cities. Afro-Caribbean and Asian men were unlikely to have retained the socio-economic position of their fathers as a result of migrating. Thus, for them at least, the promise of migration itself has yet to be fulfilled.

Conclusion
As yet, this chapter has said little about the 'identity options' of young British citizens of Asian and Afro-Caribbean origin. The very fact of British birth, or migration at a very early age, suggests that the first option is to identify with the majority community, even while retaining aspects of a special tradition and history. To some extent, this is an inevitable process regardless of the unwillingness of the majority to concede equity and the equalities of citizenship to newer arrivals of different appearance and culture. Young people from ethnic-minority groups share in the sub-cultures of youth more generally. They support the same teams in sports; they listen to the same music; they watch the same programmes on television. The differences they experience are twofold. Firstly, they carry with them a family tradition that sets them apart from the majority. Sometimes this will involve religion, or language, clothing or even the expectations of adherence to distinctive patterns of family life itself. These provide for them, as for others, a reservoir from which identity can be moulded and formed. Secondly, ethnic-minority youth are marked out by others as justifying a special response simply because of their appearance or distinctive culture. The key question is often thought to be whether differences in identity flow more from the cultural tradition or from the hostility of the majority. The answer is probably that the dichotomy is false. Culture is like a reservoir that can be drained and refilled. The key to the salience of minority culture is the reception of the majority. As long as racist patterns of exclusion and marginalization exist, then young people can never reject their past, for to do so would be to deny themselves autonomy and self-respect.

Much of the foregoing argument has been to document the extent to which labour-market participation has been affected by the response of the majority. It has also sought to suggest a less familiar thesis. Ethnic minorities in the UK were incorporated as migrant labour at a time of labour shortage and as such they have been disproportionately affected by the collapse of demand for labour, often precisely in those industries to which they were originally recruited. The struggle for equity cannot succeed unless this is recognized, and strategies for alleviation incorporated in any policy response. So far, small gains against discrimination have been offset by newly emerging inequalities in the labour market. As one wound has been staunched, others have been inflicted, and it must now be an open question as to whether the health of ethnic minority communities can survive this new onslaught. That is the key question for the future.

Notes
1. For example, the government has greatly extended an experimental initiative to redirect secondary education towards more vocational ends (the Technical and Vocational Training Initiative) and has recently announced the formation of new city technical colleges to be run by voluntary associations in partnership with local industry with funds provided by the Treasury.
2. This section is similar to Cross 1987a, p. 2.
3. See Cross 1987b for a development of this argument.
4. This section is derived from an earlier report by the present author (Cross 1986a).

References

Brown, C. (1984), *Black and White Britain: The Third PSI Survey*, London: Heinemann.

Careers Bulletin, (1978) 'Employment Problems of Young People From Ethnic Minorities', *Careers Bulletin* (Autumn), 23–28.

Courteney, G. (1983), 'Analysis of Data from the Survey of 1980–81 YOP Entrants', unpublished mimeo.

CRE (1978), *Looking for Work: Black and White School Leavers in Lewisham*, London: Commission for Racial Equality.

Cross, M. (1986a), *The Training Situation of Ethnic Minority Young People in Britain*. West Berlin: Centre for the Development of Vocational Training.

Cross, M. (1986b) 'Migration and Exclusion: Caribbean Echoes and British Realities' in Brock, C. *The Caribbean in Europe: Aspects of West Indian Experience in Britain, France and the Netherlands*, London: Frank Cass.

Cross, M. (1987a), 'Black Youth and YTS: the Policy Issues', in M. Cross and D. I. Smith (eds.), *Black Youth Futures: Ethnic Minorities and the Youth Training Scheme* Leicester: National Youth Bureau, Studies in Research.

Cross, M. (1987b), *A Cause for Concern: Ethnic Minority Youth and Vocational Training Policy*, Policy Paper in Ethnic Relations No. 9, Coventry: Centre for Research in Ethnic Relations.

Cross, M. *et al.* (1983), *Ethnic Minorities: Their Experience of YOP*, Sheffield: Manpower Services Commission.

Cross, M. and Johnson, M. J. D. (forthcoming), *Race and the Urban System* Cambridge: Cambridge University Press.

Cross, M. and Smith, D. I. (1987), *Black Youth Futures: Ethnic Minorities and the Youth Training Scheme*, Studies in Research, Leicester: National Youth Bureau.

Cross, M. and Wrench, J. (1987), 'Processing Black Youngsters: Careers Service or Disservice', Paper presented to the British Sociological Association Annual Conference.

Cross, M., Wrench, J. and Barnet, S. (1987), *Ethnic Minorities and the Careers Service: An Investigation into Processes of Assessment and Placement* Unpublished report to the Department of Employment.

Department of Employment (1982), *Labour Force Survey 1981*, London: Her Majesty's Stationery Office.

Department of Employment (1987a), 'Ethnic Origin and Economic Status', *Employment Gazette*, January.

Department of Employment (1987b), *Labour Force Survey 1985*, London: Her Majesty's Stationery Office.

Dex, S. (1981), *Black and White School Leavers: The First Five Years of Work* Department of Employment Research Paper No. 33, London: Her Majesty's Stationery Office.

Fenton, S. *et al.* (1984), *Ethnic Minorities and the Youth Training Scheme*, Research and Development Paper No. 20, Sheffield: Manpower Services Commission.

Field, S. *et al.* (1981), *Ethnic Minorities in Britain: A Study of Trends in their Position Since 1961*, Home Office Research Study No. 68, London: Her Majesty's Stationery Office.

Fowler, B. *et al.* (1977), 'Immigrant School Leavers and the Search for Work', *Sociology* 11(1), 65–68.

HMSO (1984), *Labour Force Survey, 1983*, London: Her Majesty's Stationery Office.

HMSO (1985), *A New Training Initiative: A Programme for Action*, Cmnd 8455, London: Her Majesty's Stationery Office.

HMSO (1985) *Education and Training for Young People*, Cmnd 9842, London: Her Majesty's Stationery Office.

House of Commons (10 November 1983), *Parliamentary Debates (Hansard)*, Col. 219

Houses of Commons (18 February 1986), *Written Answers*, Col. 135.

Lee, G. and Wrench, J. (1981), *In Search of a Skill*, London: Commission for Racial Equality.

Massey, D. (1984), *Spatial Divisions of Labour: Social Structures and the Geography of Production*, London: Macmillan.

MSC (1979), *Special Programmes, Special Needs; Ethnic Minorities and the Special Programmes for the Unemployed*, London: Manpower Services Commission.

MSC (1981a), *The New Training Initiative: A Consultative Document*, London: Manpower Services Commission.

MSC (1981b), *A New Training Initiative: An Agenda for Action*, London: Manpower Services Commission.

MSC (1981c), *Review of the Third Year of Special Programmes*, London: Manpower Services Commission.

MSC (1982a), *Task Group Report*, London: Manpower Services Commission

MSC (1982b), *Annual Report of the Manpower Services Commission 1981/82*, Sheffield: Manpower Services Commission

MSC (1983), *Towards an Adult Training Strategy*, Sheffield: Manpower Services Commission

MSC (1985), *Development of the Youth Training Scheme: A Report*, Sheffield: Manpower Services Commission

OPCS (1983) 'Labour Force Survey 1981: Country of Birth and Ethnic Origin', *OPCS Monitor*, 83/1.

Peach, G. C. K. (1968), *West Indian Migration to Britain*, London: Oxford University Press.

Sillitoe, K. (1980), *Young People's Employment Study: Preliminary Report No. 4*, London: Office of Population Censuses and Surveys.

Smith, D. J. (1981), *Unemployment and Racial Minorities*, London: Policy Studies Institute.

4   The Condition of Young People of Foreign Origin in France

Salvatore Palidda and Marie-Claude Muñoz

Introduction

This chapter analyzes the position of young foreigners in France so that the reader can compare their conditions with those of young people of foreign origin living in other European countries. In this context, 'young people of foreign origin' refers to the 15- to 24-year-old descendants of immigrants, who were either born in France or who immigrated at an early age. This therefore includes the grandchildren or great-grandchildren of immigrants, who may be even third- or fourth-generation descendants of the older waves of migration.

The significant number of descendants of immigrants who have acquired French nationality distinguishes the French case from that of most other European countries. This factor also complicates the authors' task. The official French statistics are based on the legal categories and concepts, which do not require detailed data on the young who have obtained French nationality or who are of a more or less remote foreign origin. Because of this, young foreigners will be dealt with on the basis of official data and available studies, and young French of foreign origin will be examined on the basis of qualitative studies from specific samples. The authors will try to demonstrate that certain typical trajectories, in particular school attendance and occupational opportunities, correspond to the legal status of young people. Until now, the role that young foreigners can play as new agents in the receiving society has generally been ignored. Instead, macro-sociological approaches, with a tendency towards theoretical and ideological rigidity, have predominated. It is not only a question of understanding immigration and social policies and general statistical trends, but also the complexity of reality reflected in the attitudes of the young. This is why social and cultural dimensions and their implications are also discussed.

Historical and legal aspects

France is one of the European countries with the longest history of immigration. Unlike other European countries, it has called on immigration not only for labour needs but also for demographical and military reasons (Bonnet 1986; Schor 1980; Milza 1985; Cordeiro 1987). Furthermore, the colonial legacy continues to place the burden on the immigration context in France. This is especially important with respect to African and north-African immigrants (Sayad 1979). France's policy of assimilation has specific ramifications for the children of immigrants. Its main instrument has been various procedures for allocating French nationality,[1] including automatic acquisition at a person's majority (Catani 1984). Despite xenophobic and racist movements having emerged at every crisis of the economic, social, political and international cycle, resulting in the rejection-explusion of immigrants, about one-third of the French population is now of foreign origin (Duroselle and Serra 1978; Milza 1985). Every wave of immigration has included a period of single male migrants, although, since as early as the turn of the century, France has also tolerated and encouraged family immigration. Thus with the *de facto* combination of official recruitment policy and the growth of chain migration, the concentration of foreign workers and their families in different areas has led to the constitution of family, village and ethnic networks. These informal networks are one of the most remarkable characteristics of the foreign population, and they still provide the socio-cultural environment for the education of the young.

By the end of the 1950s, a social hierarchy of foreigners was established. The older migratory flows (Polish, Jewish, Italian, Spanish and more recently the Portuguese) have been favoured. In the mid 1970s, an attempt was made to substitute the lowly ranked north Africans with south-east Asians.[2] As a result of this social hierarchy, young foreigners have very different educational and labour-market opportunities, depending on their national origins. In addition to cultural and educational resources, the social resources of the family and the network are often crucial for their future.

The changes from 1970 to 1980
Since the beginning of the seventies, the position of young people of foreign origin has become an important social and political issue. With its economic decline and loss of international prestige, the integration potential of France diminished considerably. The cyclical economic crisis of the seventies and eighties led to a halt in immigration, which was accompanied by an increase in illegal residents (Garson and Moulier 1985) and refugees from south east Asia continued to be welcomed into the country.

Despite efforts to encourage return, the immigrant population

Table 4.1   The share of French and foreigners in the age groups 0 to 14 years and 15 to 24 years between 1962 and 1982, per cent.

Years	1962		1968		1975		1982	
	Fr.*	For.*	Fr.	For.	Fr.	For.	Fr.	For.
0–14	96.9	3.1	95.2	4.8	92.7	7.3	91.5	8.5
15–24	95.8	4.2	95.9	4.1	94.5	5.5	93.7	6.3

*Fr. = French; For. = foreigners.
Source: INSEE (1982).

became settled and stabilized. The number of immigrant children increased in previously unknown proportions, creating a specific category in the French social texture: young foreigners. The concentration of foreign population in slums, the provisional, low-cost housing of the urban suburbs, creating what has been called a 'dynamic density' (Oriol 1984).

At the same time, a xenophobic and racist reaction began to surface, and this resulted in the murder of dozens of these young people (Ben Jelloun 1984). A mass movement also emerged, beginning at a grass roots level and growing, with the help of a variety of personalities and the media, to become one of the most important phenomena of the current French social and political situation (Leclercq 1985; Palidda and Belbahri 1987; Dubet 1987).

Data on young foreign population
Owing to family reunification and high birth-rates among couples resident in France from the sixties onwards (especially among Portuguese and north Africans), the proportion of young foreigners increased.

In 1982, foreigners comprised 6.8 per cent of the population: some 948,880 foreigners were in the 0- to 14-year-old age bracket, and some 544,160 were between 15 and 24 years. If these figures are added to those 180,000 who have obtained French nationality through specific procedures and another 130,000 born of a 'mixed' marriage (French/foreigner) (INSEE 1986), a total of more than 1.8 million people of recent foreign origin aged 0 to 24 years is reached. There are no official data on French of more or less remote foreign origin. According to some rough estimates, between 35 and 45 per cent of people from 0 to 24 years old are of more or less remote foreign origin.[3]

With respect to national origins, the share of the European nationalities who had furnished the greatest number of immigrants in the past (Italy, Poland, Spain) has decreased considerably. Apart from the Portuguese, European immigration has stopped, and most of these children are now French citizens. Among the foreign youth under 24 years of age, a little more than half are north African, about one-third European and one-tenth Asian. Specifically in the 15- to 24-year-old group, Europeans are more numerous (45 per cent) than the north Africans (38 per cent). It is the magnitude of the contingent of north-African origin which worries racists, who fear the 'degeneration' of France (Costa-Lascoux 1985).

Socio-cultural environment in urban neighbourhoods
Born in the urban slums, the provisional low-cost accommodation of the suburban public housing estates, the great majority of young of foreign origin – mainly Portuguese and north African, to a lesser extent the Italians and Spanish – grew up in conditions of poverty, in a socio-cultural ghetto: a situation similar to the poorest French. Unlike their parents, who were more willing to accept harsh living conditions with the illusion or actual prospect of returning to the country of origin after having earned a little money or even the achievement of socio-professional success, the young descendants of foreigners realize that their goals cannot be the same. Their parents' country of origin is alien or even hostile to them and France, which after all is their country, rejects them, or offers very few professional possibilities (Lefort and Nery 1985).

On the one hand, informal networks and the activities of associations support the transmission and the maintenance of value through adaptation of traditional primary structures, and the encouragement of emotional ties with the culture of origin. On the other hand, generational continuity is not always guaranteed. This is especially difficult for those who were among the most disadvantaged in their country of origin. They suffer the most from the cultural disintegration which migration causes and the diverse social upheavals occurring within the country of residence. The young seldom assume responsibilities in their parents' associations (Catani and Palidda 1987). They rarely speak their language, or adopt their traditional manners and behaviour (for example the young people of north-African origin do not adopt Islam and its rules (Etienne 1987). The identity crisis of the young of foreign origin combines elements that are common to all youth with others that are specific to themselves. In the latter case, they cannot identify with their parents' cultural references or behaviour, nor do they find the goals of their parents realistic for themselves. This rupture, which is at times dramatic and at other times more subtle, is particularly apparent among north-African youth and less obvious – but still present – among the Latins (Campani and Catani 1985; Catani 1986; Oriol 1984). The search for a more truthful representation of their situation and a clearer self-image was far more important for youth of north-African origin than for the youth from other cultural origins. This has grown into a genuine mass movement with considerable impact on the French local and national scene.

School attendance
Centralization is a key characteristic of French society. Heir of absolutist and centralized monarchical spirit, the French Republic has continued through national education and other institutions to integrate French citizens to the detriment of the regional cultures (Braudel 1986). The school system has been the Republic's most efficacious instrument. As a colonial power, France practised a policy of assimilation in its colonies. During a number of decades the same national educational policy has been used for children of immigrant workers. It was not until the 1970s that the special needs of children of foreigners were recognized by:

● Creating experimental introductory classes for non-French speakers in the first degree (circular no. IX 7037, 13 January 1970) and adaptation (transitional) classes for non-French mother-tongue in the second degree (circular no. 73 383, 2 September 1973).
● Teaching national languages in elementary school (circular no. 75 48, 8 April 1975) and in colleges (circular no. 77 345, 28 September 1977).[4]
● Establishing an inter-cultural pedagogic (circular no. 78 238, 25 July 1978).

In 1985, however, the Minister of National Education, J. P. Chevenement, re-established the teaching of national culture in elementary schools (Minister of National Education 1985). Despite their objective of universal education, French schools are very selective (Bourdieu and Passeron 1970; Baudelot and Establet 1971), and they perpetuate a high rate of educational failures among children of foreign origin as well as among working class French children (Muñoz 1979; Zirotti 1979, 1980; Boulot and Fradet 1982).

In 1982, fewer than one-third (27.4 per cent) of the respective age cohort of all young people graduated from the lycee with a baccalaureate. The majority (57 per cent) of these graduates were the sons of professionals and white-collar employees and only 10 per cent were the sons of blue collar workers. It is to this latter category that the majority of foreign workers belong (*Le Monde Dossiers et Documents* 1985). Mass education results in the augmentation of the number of diplomas while correlating with the devaluation of titles. The networks for social mobility and the most profitable studies continue to be monopolized by the privileged classes (Le Thanh Khoi 1978).

The highest unemployment rates are found among young people between 15 and 24 years of age who leave compulsory schooling without a certificate. Over 38 per cent of these young people are unemployed, as compared with 24 per cent of those with a CAP or a BEP, 19 per cent of the baccalaureates and 8 per cent of those with a degree from a university or an advanced institution of higher learning (*Grande Ecole*) (INSEE 1985).

Over one million foreign pupils are enrolled in state (95 per cent) or private (5 per cent) schools under the auspices of the Ministry of National Education. If we add to these figures those pupils attending orientation and transition (adaptation) classes (697,213 foreign pupils) they comprise altogether about 10 per cent of the total number of pupils in elementary education. They contribute, however, to almost 20 per cent of the pupils enrolled in special education for weak and slightly retarded children.

Including the transitional (adaptation) classes 383,539 foreign pupils (7 per cent of the total) are enrolled in the first and second cycles of secondary school. Of these, 6.8 per cent are in the first cycle (6th to 3rd level) but 11.4 per cent attend occupational streams (CPPN–CPA) and 17 per cent are in special education classes for the slow learners and weaker pupils. They represent 9.6 per cent of the pupils in the short second cycles (CAP, BEP) and 3.9 per cent of the total number of pupils in the long second cycle (to earn the baccalaureate)[5] (see Table 4.2).

In the first and second degree, foreign youth are over-represented in special classes designed to serve children who are backward or slightly retarded. Algerian pupils, who already belong to the most discriminated foreign community, are also the strongest contingent in these classes.

In secondary education, higher frequency of orientation into pre-vocational training in the first cycle and the short second cycle is observed than in the long second cycle (see Table 4.2b).

The distribution by educational level and cycles of pupils of the different nationalities vary according to the age and social and cultural attitudes of the immigrant communities. These factors also depend largely on the maturity of the immigration process of the groups in question.

Participation in schooling beyond compulsory (16 years) level is

Table 4.2   *Share of foreign pupils in public and private institutions in the 1985–1986 academic year.*

a. *Enrolment in institutions of the first degree (primary education)*

	Total	Foreigners as percentage of total
pre-school (2–6 years)	246 311	9.6
elementary (6–10/11 yrs)	427 941	10.6
special education	14 522	19.7

b. *Enrolment in institutions of secondary education (second degree)*

	Total	Foreigners as percentage of total
1st cycle (11/12–15/16 yrs)	236 012	6.8
CPPN–CPA (14–16 yrs)	16 041	11.4
short second cycle (13–17 yrs)	78 208	9.6
long second cycle (16–18 yrs)	47 461	3.9
special education	21 858	17.0

Source: SPRESE (1986).

related to the difficulties of integration into the labour market. This is of less concern to foreign pupils. The great majority of foreign students in French universities are not the children of immigrants, but young adults who entered France solely for their university education.

It is also important to note that, as in the past, when the school was a means of social mobility, young people of foreign origin who desire and have the opportunity to carry on relatively long schooling generally acquire French nationality. This facilitates access to fellowships, to the labour market, to professional careers, especially in the civil service (Campani, Catani, and Palidda 1983). Because of this, the data on education is incomplete; there are no statistics on the number of young who have obtained French citizenship before starting their advanced education or training.

Since data on young people who have obtained French nationality are not available, it is necessary to draw on certain case studies of specific samples, for example among the Italians (ibid.) or among the Poles (Ponty 1985). These studies note that, among those who have obtained a certain socio-economic success, the younger generation who carry on with their studies usually become French citizens. They become French not only in the legal sense, but also more like the French in their behaviour and mentality.[6]

Much has been written about the difficulties that immigrant children encounter in school. These studies usually point to the parents' low 'cultural' resources, the bad material conditions in which they live, and language problems, among other difficulties. Other factors need to be added, such as the attitudes of the parents and of the children themselves. Once more, case studies show that, for some groups, formal education is considered to be a means of social mobility. This is especially true for people of rural origins who traditionally thought school important, for example the southern Italians, Spanish, some of the north Africans and Asians. Others, however, reject school automatically. The reason for this is not only their children's lack of success, but also the value placed on apprenticeships that guarantee a profitable job, or hard work which provides social resources in the form of earnings. Social resources gained in this way combine with the mobilization of family and network resources, thus increasing the possibility of self-employment. This model might be somewhere between the spirit of the self-made man and a family project. Even though this works out for only a minority, it remains a model and a point of reference for the young. Interest in self-employment reflects a combination of dispositions found among the descendants of immigrants, such as: their distaste to become wage-earners under a boss, whether French or foreign; their rejection of the work of their parents; and a desire to make up for the pain experienced as the children of immigrants, as well as a certain spirit of individualism. If these goals cannot be realized, many young people drop out. Without a formal school diploma, they become candidates for unemployment, under-paid jobs or the individual 'resourcefulness' of somehow finding their way, even into delinquency. Finally, the economic situation during the last decade in France has meant that schooling and occupational training does not always lead to the appropriate job.

The labour market

Changes in the residence permit regulations for foreigners were made in 1984. Most young foreigners now fulfil one of the necessary conditions for receiving an automatic residence permit at the age of 16; this allows them to live and work in the country. It is valid ten years and is automatically renewed. Foreigners under 25 years of age represent about 70 per cent of the total population newly entering the job market annually, and they are one of the most important sources of legal replenishment of the foreign work force. In general, foreign youths enter the job market earlier than French youth: this seems to result from the fact that most young foreigners do not continue studies after compulsory education, and are mostly found in areas of education that lead to an early entry into employment.

The context of the French labour market An analysis of the recent evolution of the French job market is given in a special issue of the INSEE review *Economie et Statistique* (1986). The most significant findings are that:

The intermediate situations, the precarious jobs only form a small part of the job market, but they are of great importance in the hiring of workers, in the production of recurrent unemployment, and for many young ... In the last four years, the increase of part-time jobs and the decrease of full-time jobs balance each other. Other phenomena are quickly occurring: under-employment has doubled. The insertion of the young, often intermittent or unadapted, only occurs through dequalification. In these situations, which are often near to each other or overlap, the drawing of boundaries, at a given time, between work, unemployment and inactivity is becoming more and more conventional, to a point in which, far from full employment or stable, full-time activity, one comes to recognize the existence of a halo or a fringe that would constitute a new solution to the economic crisis.

About 70 per cent of the net job creation (between March 1985 and March 1986) came from the various training periods (407,000 paid and registered beneficiaries, of which 200,000 TUC – *Travaux d'Utilite Collective* (work of collective benefit) created by the Fabius administration for the young. About 59 per cent of the beneficiaries earn less than 2,000 francs a month (less than half the minimum guaranteed salary (SMIC)) and 20 per cent earn between 2,000 and 4,500 francs. Some 52 per cent of the beneficiaries work part-time and almost two-thirds are employed by the state or local administration.

Furthermore, work contracts signed for a definite (short) period have increased 23 per cent in one year; between 1982 and 1986 part-time jobs have increased by 530,000, while full-time permanent jobs have decreased by 550,000. Between March 1985 and March 1986, 37 per cent of the people hired in secure jobs were aged under 25 – this age cohort representing 13 per cent of the active population. Meanwhile, 40 per cent of the layoffs for economic reasons hit workers aged more than 50, who represent 17 per cent of the active population. 'Vulnerability, precariousness, mobility have become the main words meaning adjustment to the needs of the economy' (Lebaube 1987). In March 1986, 1.4 million people (6.4 per cent of the actives) occupied 'intermediate' positions, while waiting for a more stable job, that is 227,000 more than the previous year. (Between 1968 and 1975, this group comprised 600,000 on average.) Under-employment affected 0.4 to 0.5 million people (this level was double that of four years previously). The young, especially, were under-employed on average for a year before finding another job or unemployment. The level of unemployment increased for all young, and also depended on what diplomas were obtained, being lowest for those who had obtained the baccalaureat (end of high school). One-third of those aged 15 to 25 were still at school, one-third held a job, one-ninth were out of work and one-twelfth occupied an intermediate situation (apprenticeship, alternating training periods, TUC). The most difficult situation is for those aged 18 to 21, of whom 34 per cent were at school, 27 per cent working, 9 per cent 'precarious activity' and 15 per cent unemployed.

The employed

The 1982 census gives only a very general picture of the activity rate of young foreigners. No information is available on occupational categories or economic activity according to age, nor is there a breakdown according to nationality. The only information available is that, from a total of over 500,000 young people in this age group, 217,000 are registered as employed or actively seeking employment. Their mean activity rate is about 40 per cent (Table 4.3).

The rate of unemployment is higher for foreigners than natives in each age group and for both sexes. Two-thirds of the unemployed foreigners are men and one-third are women. Over 67,000 young foreigners between 15 and 24 years old are seeking work with a mean unemployment rate of 31 per cent. In this case, it is the 15 to 19 year olds who have the highest rate of unemployment: 41 per cent; one half of the young women economically active in this age bracket are unemployed.

For comparative purposes, the unemployment rate among French nationals of the same age group is lower (22 per cent; 17 per cent

Table 4.3.   The activity rate of foreigners 15 to 24 years of age in 1982.

		both sexes	male	female
1.	Total foreigners 15 to 24 years	544,160 (100%)	277,300 (100%)	266,860 (100%)
2.	Economically active among 15 to 24 year old foreigners	217,200 (39.9%)	128,520 (46.3%)	88,680 (33.2%)
3.	Employed among the economically active	149,800	94,280	55,520
4.	The unemployed among the economically active	67,400	34,240	33,160
5.	The Unemployment Rate (Categ. 4 in rel. to cat. 2)	(31.0%)	(26.6%)	(37.4%)

Source: Lebon, (1985), based on the 1982 Census

Table 4.4   The rate of activity according to sex by age groups for foreigners

Years	Total population	Total number in work	Percentage in work	Total number unemployed	Percentage unemployed
Males					
15–19	144 540	34 980	24.2	12 200	34.9
20–24	132 550	93 540	70.5	2 040	23.6
Females					
15–19	133 100	23 500	17.7	11 920	50.7
20–24	133 760	65 180	48.7	21 240	32.6

Source: INSEE (1982)

for men and 27 per cent for women). It is also lower (11 per cent) among the adult (over 25 years) foreign population (10 per cent for men and 15 per cent for women) (Lebon 1985). This must be seen in the general context of more than 2.5 million unemployed in September 1986, of whom nearly a million are under 25 years old. (A total of 300,000 foreigners of all ages are unemployed.)

Until the beginning of the 1980s, Algerians were two to three times more likely to be unemployed than Portuguese (who had a comparable rate of activity). In 1986, the situation changed among young people under 25; unemployment is slightly higher for Portuguese than for Algerians (22.4 per cent for Portuguese and 21.4 per cent for Algerians). Both of these populations have a very low level of educational achievement, and with the general low level of job vacancies, they both suffer from similar problems of unemployment. One study (CEREQ *see* Amat 1984) indicates that the unemployment rate among young foreigners without educational qualifications (level VI) is no higher than that of the young French with the same educational level.

Nationality, however, seems to be a greater disadvantage for young foreigners, irrespective of sex, who participated in a short training cycle leading to no recognized degree (level V). The unemployment rate of young foreigners who reach level V (short training with the allocation of a CAP or BEP degree) is lower for males than for females, and the gap shrinks between foreigners and French. Generally, young foreigners are excluded from work in the public-service sector because of their nationality.

Although young foreigners are as unlikely to be involved in the non-commercial service sector as the older foreign generation, they tend to resemble the young French more in their chances of being employed in the *marchand* service sector. They are also closer to native youth with respect to frequency of employment in construction.

These data illustrate the growing importance of the service sector and a generally distinctive pattern of sectoral participation among young foreigners, which differentiates them from their parents' generation. It is important to note that any comparison between those two categories of people must take into consideration the vast transformations that have taken place in the French economic system in recent years (new technologies, robotization, sytems of information, the destruction and totally new reconstruction of some sectors of activity). These changes have particularly affected economic sectors and regions in which the presence of a foreign work force was traditionally strong: mining, textiles, manufacturing in general, and even the heavy industries, such as the steel and car industry. Because of the difficulty in making comparisons

Table 4.5 *Labour market participation according to sector of activity, nationality and age, per cent*

	French 15–24 years	Foreigners 15–24 years	Foreigners 25 years and over
Industry	26.7	30.7	30.0
Construction and public works	9.4	15.35	23.25
Tertiaire merchand	45.3	40.5	29.2
Tertiaire non-marchand[1]	13.7	9.35	9.05

Agriculture only occupies 4 to 5% of the activities in each of the categories.

Source: Lebon (1985).

according to nationality and age groups with respect to occupational position, it is necessary to refer to case studies which the authors have carried out. These indicate:

(a)   that some young foreigners have more difficulties in access to the job market than their parents did. They are either destined to occupy the less qualified and the less well-paid jobs, or they are obliged to accept insecure, occasional jobs, often in the fast-growing informal economy, which is becoming more and more common in France (Gr~ffe and Archambault 1984; Palidda 1987);

(b)   Others are condemned to unemployment, the alternative lying either between participation in some token governmental measures (various training programmes and so on) or in some form of illegal activity (Malewska-Peyre 1982; Catani and Verney 1986; Dubet 1987).

Using data on the presence of foreigners in certain sectors of economic activity, Lebon (1985) asserts that there exists: 'a certain reproduction of the foreign workforce, which is more apparent for young men than for young women...' As has been pointed out earlier, this observation also suffers from the fact that it cannot take into account those young people who have obtained French nationality. Despite this, many studies show that there is no reproduction of the work force, in the strict sense of the term, because even if, at the more global level, young foreigners are found to have the same level of qualification as the preceding generation,

Table 4.6   *Economically active Spanish women according to age and sector of activity, per cent*

Sector	Spanish females under 25 years	Spanish females 25 years and over
Industry	31.46	17.5
Marchand	52.09	42.4
Non-marchand	8.39	35.6

Source: INSEE (1982).

they seldom adopt the occupation of their parents. Thus, it is rare to find the son of a train cleaner or a street sweeper in the same occupation as his father, or the daughter of a daily help doing the same as her mother. In the same sense, the son of a miner, a worker in textiles or in the car industry more and more rarely enters the same occupation as his father. This observation has less to do with the elimination of a certain number of jobs that their parents filled and more to do with the attitudes of the younger generation who desire another style of life to that of their parents, even though they may accept, at least in the beginning, worse working conditions. This is seen more clearly if data for gender and nationality is examined. For example, only 8 per cent of Spanish women under 25 years old are employed in the service branch (including domestic services), but more than one-third of those over 25 are found in this branch. This phenomenon is also observed among Portuguese women. A disaffection with trade services (hotels, restaurants and so on) in favour of employment in the commercial sector may be seen. To summarize: this means that young Spanish women are no longer willing to work in domestic services (*services non-marchands*), nor in the menial service jobs in the hotel and restaurant area (*services marchands*).

This evolution constitutes a radical rupture with the parent generation, and as a consequence it leads to an increased presence of young foreigners under 25 in commerce and even in the industrial sector (especially in the production of consumer goods) (Muñoz 1986). As a result, since the descendants of Spanish and Portuguese immigrants do not wish to take the jobs their parents held in certain areas, the need for clandestine (illegal) workers is not likely to disappear in the future. This eventuality may well happen in all developed countries (Reyneri 1985).

In this context, particular mention should be made of two 'sectors' of activity-offering jobs at least to a minority of the young, which may become models or a new point of reference for them:

(a) the development of self-employment (craftsmanship, small trade and industry) may at times be considered true ethnic business, especially among certain groups. If it is not extensive enough to provide an ethnic business sector, it may still be important for socio-economic networks which train the next generation to carry on and take over;

(b) the development of the so-called 'social economy' providing jobs in partnerships, associations and co-operatives (*Cashiers francais* 1985). Even if this area is well supported, it does not seem to constitute a real hope for the young, who often do not even know it exists.

Owing to the growth of youth unemployment since 1975, the various governments have taken measures to protect employment. For example, during the last decade, the participation of young foreigners in the various training projects has doubled (from 6 to 13 per cent). In general, the rate of participation in training programmes is lower for young foreigners born in their country of origin (25 per cent) than for those born in France (30 per cent). Also, young women are always less represented in the different types of training programmes than young men.

These training programmes do not guarantee employment, and the majority of young foreigners find a job without any help from the state (Chevallier 1986).

The governmental, institutional and administrative treatment of the problems posed by young people of foreign origin

The public administration had been aware for a while of the problems posed by the descendants of immigrants, but it was not until 1970 that it seriously started to seek solutions. At that time, health, housing and school problems were the predominant concerns, whereas, in the late seventies and at the beginning of the eighties, socio-economic and cultural problems exploded. This was either because no one had cared earlier, or because the economic crisis occurred in France during a period when a serious disequilibrium existed between peak branches and an outdated system of production. Until then, the old production system had been expected to yield high profits with a low cost work force.

Already before the arrival of a socialist government (May 1981), the administration had thought it sufficient to provide financial aid for social assistance and community organizations, semi-public and private (mostly religious) groups. Nevertheless, no changes occurred on the socio-economic or educational level. The socialists favoured 'social treatment' of the problem, while economic measures ('Work Agreement', incentives to hire young people, 'TUC' (work for collective benefit)) did not achieve the desired effects.

France has not experienced the serious riots that occurred in England, but there have been xenophobic and racist movements and frequent local neighbourhood incidents and community tensions. The government counted on 'social work' to calm down the young with special programmes for the 'hot summer', mass leisure activities, help for associations and private radio stations, concert happenings (the Woodstock model) and incentives to create an élite leadership for the young, that is representatives with whom local administrators, the private and public organizations and politicians could initiate a continuous dialogue.

This programme indeed managed to form an élite, with a proliferation of associations for young people (especially north Africans), and local movements were channelled into one large mass national movement. From this emerged the demonstrations of the 'Beurs' (young north African descendants) in 1983, the 1984 'Convergences' movement, 'SOS Racism', and so on. A somewhat 'tame' result, among other reasons because of the divisions produced by competition between active organizations to take control (the Left leaders, the Catholic Church and others who considered themselves true representatives of foreign youth, particularly of the young of north African descent).

This élite established itself as a privileged representative, and the results of the dialogue clearly proved to be inadequate, since labour opportunities for the great majority of the young could not be provided. This put the young descendants of immigrants right back where they started.

Since the establishment of the Chirac government in 1986, the situation has not improved as far as racial animosities and xenophobia are concerned. Even though a revival of the economy was promised, which should benefit all the young, unemployment is higher and the chances of finding a job remain depressed.

Meanwhile, the associations that flourished in the 1983–86 period are now disappearing, whilst the gap between the élite and the young foreigners widens.[8] This gap is a problem considering the possible actions that might be taken by the young people who cannot accept the difficulty of the present situation and are seeking solutions.

Conclusions
France took recourse to immigration at a time when there was not

only an economic requirement for temporary labourers, but also a need for men and women to re-establish its demographic balance, personnel for its national army, and population for certain regions of the country. However, the productive structure of the decade between 1970 and 1980, and the whole range of economic activities, no longer require a mass of foreign manpower. Moreover, no one foresaw that the mass of workers once recruited and sought during the 1960s would produce a new and important component of youth in France during a phase when the labour market was no longer benefiting from dynamic growth. These young people, born, educated and socialized in France, are destined to stay; return is not a real prospect for them, and they rarely adhere to a myth of return.

Current debate centres around reforming the nationality law, which would abolish the automatic acquisition of French nationality at 18 years of age for young people born in France of foreign parents. This would be a breach in the assimilationist policy of French traditions, since nearly one-third of the total population has foreign origins. The access to French nationality, and the rights and liberties that are attached to this, has greatly contributed to the integration of the preceding migratory flows. The adjournment of this proposal, however, reflects the resistance it meets on all sides. It is also very unlikely that France will abandon its traditional attitude with respect to immigrants and their children. Opposing this wave of xenophobia, defence of national interests and French identity, numerous experts, politicians and civil servants affirm that young people of foreign origin constitute 'an opportunity for the future of France'. If the reader looks beyond the instrumental or demagogical (or even ideological) use of this expression, he will see that it is upheld essentially with arguments of a demographic order. Any other arguments in support of this assertion are fuzzy and are not based on any general consensus (about, for example, the cultural enrichment foreign youth may offer).

Little official attention is given to the socio-economic dynamics produced by immigrants, for example their self-employment and involvement in the unofficial economy which France has recently found so beneficial. Nor is much notice taken of their function as a cultural and economic vehicle with respect to relations with their countries of origin. Perhaps it is in this area that young people of foreign origin offer France the 'opportunity for tomorrow', an opportunity to re-strengthen their ties with the countries around the Mediterranean.

Young foreigners will eventually find a place, be it good or bad, in French society. However, it is necessary to raise questions about where they will be situated with respect to the present changes and those to come. Although the evidence is not sufficiently conclusive to allow any certain predictions, it is possible to draw up some tentative hypotheses which suggest a probable development. One likely eventuality is the segmentation of this generation via the dual economy. While some may enter sectors in transformation, with a future, others may live on the margins of society, as obsolete remainders of the past, the 'Third World led to the West' (sweat-shops, and so on), or they may slide into more or less organized criminality. From this point of view, the condition and future of young people of foreign origins is not that much different from that of the young French who live in similar environments.

Notes

1. French nationality can be obtained: (a) by naturalization – of the children also; (b) by marriage to a French spouse; (c) 'automatically', in the sense that a child born in France of foreign parents is French when he reaches 18 years of age, if during the previous year he did not waive the right to French nationality; (d) every child who has a French parent is French-born; and (e) because of the *jus soli* the Algerians born in Algeria before independence (1963) are French.

   The question of nationality has always been seen as critical when the choice of stabilization is made. To this is owed the very high reduction in foreign population coming from old and important countries of emigration to France: Italy, Spain and Poland. Around the end of the 1970s, the interest in obtaining French nationality decreased, but by the mid 1980s it seems to have returned. According to a study done by Catani, (1984), between 90 and 95 per cent of children born in France of foreign parents automatically obtain French nationality under article 44 of the Nationality Code, when they reach majority. This article is now under review in a draft bill of the Chirac government.

2. A very useful analysis of the historical evolution of the economic stake and social problems of immigration in France is proposed by Cordeiro (1984), see especially 'the Giscard policy' (pp. 87–1.4). During this period, incentives and expulsions were reintroduced in order to encourage immigrants to leave, all measures directed more specifically towards north Africans. Meanwhile France received south-east-Asian refugees, who quickly became numerous, but were seldom present in the branches of activity where the north African population was predominant, that is building and public works, and industry.

3. Between 1975 and 1982, the foreign population in France has increased by 7 per cent. An increase has also been registered in French of foreign origin. One foreigner out of three is under 20 years of age, and 60 per cent of foreigners of this age are born in France. Some 48 per cent of foreigners are European, and 43 per cent African (nine-tenths of the Africans are north Africans). According to official statistics, for the first time foreigners are less economically active than the French: 42 per cent against 43 per cent (70 per cent against 78 per cent for the population aged 20 to 54); 88 per cent of foreign men and 91 per cent of French men are active; 42 per cent of foreign women and 65.5 per cent of French women. Beyond the effects of the growing young foreign population and the acquisition of French nationality by numerous young of foreign origin, these data do not seem reliable because they cannot take into account the undeclared or informal activities (for example domestic work of foreign women). Some 93.5 per cent of foreigners live in an ordinary household.

4. Instruction in the language of origin (three hours a week) as part of the elementary

school timetable is given by foreign teachers recruited and paid by their own governments. Bilateral agreements have been made with Portugal, Italy, Tunisia, Spain, Morrocco, Yugoslavia, Turkey and Algeria. If this instruction cannot be included in the school timetable, provisions are made for extra-curricular tuition, in the establishments of *L'education national* (public education).

When they reach the second degree, the children of immigrants may select their language of origin to study as a first or second modern language. Failing this, they may follow parallel courses run by the foreign authorities, designed with only children of the relevant mother tongue in mind.

5. CPPN (*classes preprofessionnelles de niveau* pre-professional level classes) and CPA (*classes preparatoires a l'apprentissage*/preparatory classes for apprenticeship) are classes of a pre-occupational nature which lead to technical training and apprenticeships. Except in the rarest of cases, they never lead to the CAP (*certificat d'aptitude professionnelle* – see below).

Children destined for apprenticeships are steered towards these classes via the CFA (*Centres de Formation d'Apprentis*/apprenticeship training centres) with no real hope of training or true occupational qualifications. The direction of young people towards these classes takes place at the end of the fifth degree: 14- to 15-year-old pupils are steered towards the CPPN, and those over 15 towards the CPA.

The *second cycle court* (short second cycle) is taught in LEP *Lycees d'enseignement professionels*/secondary schools) and prepares for three occupational diplomas:

- CAP (*certificat d'aptitude professionnelle*/certificate of professional aptitude) Workman or employee degree, awarded at the end of a three-year term initiated at the age of 13 to 15 years.

- BEP (*brevet d'etudes professionnelles*/degree of professional studies) Workman or qualified employee degree, awarded at the end of a two-year term initiated at the age of 15 years and including more technical instruction.

- CEP (*certificat d'etudes professionnelles*/certificate of occupational studies) Workman diploma, awarded at the end of a one-year term initiated at the age of 15, after completing the fifth degree or the CPPN. This diploma does not involve an examination and is geared towards employment in specialized types of labouring.

The *second cycle long* (long second cycle) is taught in lycées, from the second class to the 'terminal' (final class) and prepares for the *baccalaureat de l'enseignement general et de l'enseignement technique* (school-leaving certificate of general education and technical education), and also for the BT (*brevet de technicien*/ technical degree), awarded at the end of a three-year term.

6. Even though they represent only a minority in the population considered, in some networks they represent important proportions. For example, 30 per cent of the actives originating from Latium are found in independent activities or in managerial positions; 60 per cent are qualified or highly qualified workers, while only 10 per cent hold the lowest qualifications – and wages (Palidda 1982).

7. *Tertiaire marchand* are services in commerce, banks, transportation, communication, trades and crafts and hotels and restaurants. *Tertiaire non-marchand* are services in administration, public and domestic services.

8. This élite, in its search of 'institutionalization', is now seeking to give the young a political weight, through enlistment on the election registers, participation in the next presidential elections, and so on.

References

Amat, F. (1984), 'La situation des jeunes d'origine étrangère à la sortie de l'école', *Formation-Emploi*, 8.

Amat, F. (1985), 'Itinéraire dans le dispositif de formation et situation à la sortie des stages', *Formation-Emploi*, **9**.

Aventur, F. (1985), 'Les stages de formation alternée des jeunes de 16 à 18 ans', *Dossiers Statistiques du Travail et de l'Emploi*, **12/13**.

Baudelot, C. and Establet, R. (1971), *L'école Capitaliste en France* Paris: Maspero.

Belorgey, J. M. (1984), *Rapport d'Information sur la Politique de l'Immigration*, Assemblée Nationale.

Ben Jelloun, T. (1984) *Hospitalité Francaise*, Paris: Seuil.

Betbeder, M. C. (1985), 'Embauche des jeunes, ça repart. Enquête', *Le Monde de l'Education*, December.

Bonnet, J–Ch. (1966), *Pouvoirs Publics Français et l'Immigration dans l'Entre Deux Guerres*, These d'état, Lyon:

Boulot, S. and Fradet, D. (1982), *Taxinomie Scolaire, Faire Parler les Statistiques*, Saint Cloud: Centre de Recherches et d'Etudes pour la Diffusion du Français.

Bourdieu, P. and Passeron, J. C. (1970), *La Reproduction*, Editions de Minuit.

Braudel, F. (1986), *L'identité de la France*, Paris: Gallimard.

Campani, G. (1983), 'Identité et représentation dans l'analyse du contenu' in *Status of Migrants' Mother Tongues*, Strasbourg: European Science Foundation.

Campani, G. (1983b), 'Les réseaux italiens en France et la famille', *Peuples Méditerranéens/Mediterranean Peoples*, **24**.

Campani, G. (ed.) (1981), *Per un approccio regionale dell'immigrazione italiana in Francia*, Rome: Ministero de Lavoro-Instituto Santi.

Campani, G. (ed.) (1982), *Le Comunità e i gruppi d'immigrati italiani in Francia*, Rome: Santi Editrice.

Campani, G., Catani, M. and Palidda, S. (1983), *I giovani italiani in Francia*, Rome: Santi Editrice.

Campani, G. and Catani, M. (1985), 'Les réseaux associatifs italiens en France et les jeunes', *Revue Européenne des Migrations Internationales*, **2**.

Catani, M. (1983), 'L'identité et les choix relatifs aux systèmes de valeurs', *Peuples Méditerranéens/Mediterranean Peoples*, **24**.

Catani, M. (ed.)(1984), *Analyse des motivations des personnes qui déclinent la nationalité française par le jeu de l'art*, 45 du Code de la Nationalité, Paris: Ministere du Travail.

Catani, M. (1986), 'Un'ipotesi di lettura delle relazioni tra genitori e figli; emigrazione, individualizzazione e reversibilità orientata delle scelte', in S. and A.Di Carlo (eds.) *I Iuoghi dell'identità*, Milan: Angeli.

Catani, M. and Verney, P. (1986), *Se ranger des Voitures, Les "Mecs" de Jaricourt et l'Auto-école*, Paris: Meridiens Klincksieck.

Catani, M. and Palidda, S. (eds.) (1987), *Le Role du Mouvement Associatif dans l'Evolution des Communautes Immigrées*, Paris: Ministère du Travail, Fonds d'Action Sociale.

Chevallier, F. (1986), 'Situation d'ensemble des jeunes issus de l'immigration', *Actualités-Migrations*, **109**.

Cohen, P. and Garin, C. (1986). 'Le bilan de la gauche', *Le Monde de l'Education*, February.

Cordeiro, A. (1987), *L'Immigration*, Paris: Maspero.

Costa-Lascoux, J. (1982). 'La condition des jeunes d'origine étrangère; approche de sociologie juridique', in J. Marangé and A. Lebon (eds.), *L'insertion des Jeunes d'Origine Etrangère dans la Société Française*, Paris: La Documentation Française.

Costa-Lascoux, J. (1985), 'Filiations et dépendances institutionnelles: les secondes générations', *Revue Européenne des Migrations Internationales*, **2**.

Costa-Lascoux, J. and E. Temime (eds.) (1984), *Les Algériens en France*, Paris: Publisud.

Dubet, F. (1987), *La Galère: Jeunes en Survie*, Paris: Fayard.

Duroselle, J. B. and Serra, E. (eds.) (1978), *L'Emigrazione Italiana in Francia Prima del 1914* Milan: Angeli.

Etienne, B. (1987), *L'islamisme radical*, Paris: Hachette.

Freyssinet, J. (1984), *Le Chômage*, Paris: La Découverte.

Galland, O. (1985), *Les Jeunes*, Paris: La Découverte.

Garson, J. P. and Moulier, Y. (1985), *Les Clandestins*, Paris: Publisud.

Greffe, X, and Archambault, E. (1984), *Les Économies Non Officielles*, Paris: La Découverte.

INSEE (1982), *Les Etrangers* (Recensement Général de la Population de 1982), Paris: La Documentation Française.

INSEE (1985), *Enquête sur l'Emploi*, March.

INSEE (1986), *Economie et Statistique*, numéro spécial sur l'emploi et le chômage, November/December.

Lebaube, A. (1987), 'Les données sociales 1987' in *Le Monde*, 2 October, 37.

Lebon, A. (1985), 'Les caractéristiques de l'emploi des jeunes étrangers', in an unpublished paper delivered at a conference of the GRECO 13 (Groupement de Recherches Cordonnées sur les Migrations Internationales), Centre Nationale de la Recherche Scientifique: Lille

Lefort, F. and Nery, M. (1985), *Emigre dans mans pays*, Paris: CIEMI Harmattan.

Le Thanh, Khoï (1978), *Jeunesse Exploitée, Jeunesse Perdue?'* Paris: Presses Universitaires de France.

Maillat, D, (1985), 'Labour market dynamics and international migration'; unpublished paper delivered at the International Population Conference, Florence, June.

Malewska-Peyre, H. (ed.) (1982), *Crise d'Identité et Déviance Chez les Jeunes Immigrés*. Paris: La Documentation Française.

Marangé, J. and Lebon, A. (eds.) (1982), *L'Insertion des Jeunes d'Origine Etrangère dans la Société Française*, Paris: La Documentation Française.

Massot, J. (1985), 'Français par le sang, Français par la loi, Français par le choix', *Revue Européene des Migrations Internationales*, 2.

Milza, P. (1985), 'Un siècle d'immigration en France', *XX Siècle*, 7.

Monde (le) (1985), 'L'école publique aujourd' hui', *Dossiers et Documents*, **126,** October

Muñoz, M. C. (1979a), *L'Incidence de la Scolarisation sur l'Accès au Marché du Travail des Adolescents Etrangers*, Paris: Commission Nationale pour les Etudes Interethniques.

Muñoz, M. C. (1979b), *Young Immigrants - no way out*, London: North East London Polytechnic, Centre for Studies in Counselling.

Muñoz, M. C. (1981), 'Les jeunes algériens sur le marché du travail français', in *L'Émigration Maghrébine en Europe: Exploitation ou Coopération?*, Algiers: Centre de Recherche en Economie Appliquée

Muñoz, M. C. (1986), 'L'insertion professionnelle des jeunes étrangers en France, Les Espagnols', in *La Insercion Laboral de los Jovenes Españoles en Alemania y Francia*, Madrid: Instituto Español de Emigracion - Grupo de Estudios Sobre Emigracion.

Noiriel, G. (1984), Longwy, *Immigrés et Prolétaires (1880–1980)*, Paris: Presses Universitaires de France.

Oriol, M. (ed.) (1984), *Les Variations de l'Identité*, Nice: Institut d'Etudes et de Recherches Interethniques et Interculturelles.

Palidda, S. (1982), 'Rapporto di ricerca sugli originari della Valle di Comino', in G. Campani (ed.) 1982, op. cit.

Palidda, S. (1985a), 'Notes sur les parcours de la migration italienne', *Peuples Méditerranéens/Mediterranean Peoples*, **31/32**.

Palidda, S. (1985b), 'Les Italiens et la Formation', *Etudes Migrations*, **78**.

Palidda, S. (1985c), *La Communauté Locale et les Jeunes à Pierrelaye*, Paris: Agence pour le développement des relations interculturelles.

Palidda, S. (1987), 'Le phénomène mafioso ', *Temps Modernes* February.

Pallida, S. (1988), 'Mutations et immigration: ethnicité, ethnic business ou simple rentabilisation des ressources specifiques au peau economique et politique, entre formel et informel?', unpublished paper presented at a conference of GRECO

13 (Groupement de Recherches Coordonnées sur les Migrations Internationales), Vaucresson: Centre National de la Recherche Scientifique, January.

Ponty, J. (1985), *Les Polonais en France*, Paris: thése d'état.

Reyneri, E. (1979), *La catena migratoria*, Bologne: Il Mulino.

Reyneri, E. (1985), 'Migrations et segmentation du marché de l'emploi', unpublished paper presented at the International Population Conference, Florence, June.

Rose, J. (1985), 'Les jeunes et l'emploi', *Projet*, **194**.

Sayad, A. (1977) 'Les trois âges de l'immigration algérienne en France', *Actes de la Recherche en Sciences Sociales*, June.

Sayad, A. (1979), 'Les enfants illégitimes', *Actes de la Recherche en Sciences Sociales*, March.

Sayad, A. (1981), 'La naturalisation, ses conditions sociales et sa signification chez les immigrés algériens', in *Recherches sur les Migrations Internationales*, **3**, **4-5**, Groupement de Recherches coordonnées sur les migrations internationales, Centre National de la Recherche Scientifique,.

Sayad, A. (1984), 'Etat, nation et immigration: l'ordre national à l'épreuve de l'immigration', *Peuples Méditerranéens/Mediterranean Peoples*, **27/28**.

Schor, R. (1980), *L'Opinion Française et les Etrangers en France (1919-1939)*, Nice: thése d'état.

Schwartz, B. (1981), *L'insertion professionnelle et sociale des jeunes*. (Rapport au Premier Ministre), Paris: La Documentation Française.

SPRESE, Ministère de l'Education Nationale (1986), 'Les élèves de nationalité étrangère scolarisés en 1985–86 dans les établissements publics et privés des premier et second degrés', *Note d'Information*, **86-44**, November.

Zirotti, J P (1979), *La Scolarisation des Enfants de Travailleurs Immigrés. Vol. I, Evaluation, Sélection et Orientations Scolaires Analyse d'un Processus)*, Monograph, Nice: Centre Associé de Formation sur Relations Interculturelles.

Zirotti, J. P. (1980), *La Scolarisation des Enfants de Travailleurs Immigrés. Vol 2. Taxinomies et Situations Scolaires (Le Cadre de la Scolarisation dans l'Enseignement Primaire)*, Monograph, Nice: Centre Associé de Formation sur Relations Interculturelles.

Readers may also like to refer to these journals: *Peuples Méditerranéens/Mediterranean People*, *Revue Européene des Migrations Intrenationales*, *Temps Modernes*, *Etudes Migrations*, *Actes de la Recherche en Sciences Sociales*, and the publications of *Centre d'Information et d'Etudes sur les Migrations Internationales* and *l'Harmattan*.

5 Work and the Second Generation: the Descendants of Migrant Workers in the Federal Republic of Germany

Czarina Wilpert

Posing the problem

Two to three decades after the recruitment of their parents, a second and third generation of foreigners are growing up and reaching adulthood in Germany. Numerous uncertainties surround their current status, their own aspirations and their potential future. Whether born in Germany or having joined their parents at an earlier or later stage, they are neither considered to be what may be strictly defined as immigrants nor yet true ethnic minorities. 'Here for good' (Castles *et al.* 1984); they remain foreigners without a legitimate right to citizenship. As early as 1975, some politicians, worried about the explosion of a 'social time bomb', appealed for measures to secure their 'integration' (Bodenbender 1977). However, no fundamental change in policy concerning the status of foreign workers and their descendants has been enacted since recruitment was stopped in 1973.

Given their institutional marginality and their poor employment opportunities, some analyses of young foreigners in the 1980s foresee the reproduction of an immigrant-labour force (OECD 1981; Widgren, 1985). This line of argument implies that the descendant of 'guest workers' may continue to fill what, according to the dual-labour-market theory, is considered a permanent need for workers for its secondary segment (Piore 1979). This chapter will discuss some tendencies that lead to questions on such clear-cut theorizing about the current and future position of the descendants of foreign workers. In the process, it will be necessary to sort out a number of factors that interact and, at times, have contradictory implications.

One version of the dual-labour-market theory (ibid.) thoroughly studies the conditions that have to be met for the reproduction of a 'second generation' of migrant labour who would fill the same labour-market functions as their parents. The key elements that differentiate migratory from indigeneous labour centre on the migrants' instrumental attitude towards work and their temporary time-perspective, which makes it possible for them to accept jobs that are unattractive to the natives. It is noteworthy that Piore's arguments about the need for migrant labour require an understanding of the meaning of work in any society, the hierarchy of jobs within the economy, and the role of settlement and community formation in the evaluation of worthwhile jobs. Accordingly, the special suitability of a migrant worker to perform certain jobs stems from his function as an outsider, which makes him willing temporarily to perform tasks recognized as low ranking outside of his own community. Once settlement begins, a community begins to form, social relations become stabilized, and the point of reference changes from the community left behind to the new community in formation abroad. Taken in the strict sense, this argument would mean that the emergence of a 'second generation' in itself implies some form of settlement, and their settlement would disqualify them as candidates for the secondary segment of the dual-labour market. Without going into all aspects of this controversial theoretical approach here, it should be emphasized that the objective in this chapter is to address the issue of the particular characteristics of foreign workers, the qualities that make them suitable for the secondary segment of the labour market, and the context that fosters the reproduction of these characteristics rather than proving the existence or form of a dual or segmented labour market.

In Germany, the 'problem' of the second generation is often viewed as a Turkish problem. Slightly more than one-half of the almost one million foreign youths under the age of 16 are of Turkish nationality. Being a descendant of a foreign worker has repercussions for all 'guest' worker nationalities; nevertheless, some nationalities occupy a more disfavourable position than others. The most apparent distinction between nationalities is that not all foreign-worker groups have the same legal position. Workers who originate from European Economic Community (EEC) countries have a privileged status: with the exception of the right to vote, they have the same legal rights as German citizens. In addition, in the public mind, there exist different images of the various national groups, and, consequently, in the extent of receptiveness they are shown. The greatest social distance is expressed towards the Turkish population.

The author's research focuses primarily on the life histories and subjective future aspirations of the children of the Turkish and Yugoslav workers in Germany. Their individual histories are, of course, intertwined with the larger collective process of worker recruitment, family-migration conditions, and their social and institutional reception in the Federal Republic. Some aspects of the conditions they face are shared with their parents – especially their foreignness and the common goal of the migration venture. Other conditions, such as the rapid transformations of the form and meaning of work and the insecurity about the future of occupations, they share with young Germans. This chapter focuses primarily on young descendants of Turkish migrants in Germany and begins with a review of the context and conditions that constrain and stimulate their visions of the future.

Starting from this basis, three main questions arise. The first has to do with the status of foreign workers and their families within German society. It involves an analysis of the institutional conditions for membership, which might encourage or hinder change in reference groups from the society of origin to the community in formation abroad. The second question asks whether the offspring of foreign workers inherit their parents' jobs. To answer this, it will be necessary to analyze the objective indicators of the occupational position of the 15- to 25-year-old descendants of foreign workers today, relative to the first generation a decade or more ago, and relative to their indigenous peers. Moreover, since the major criteria for suitability for the secondary sector of the labour market centres on the meaning that the work a person does holds for that individual, the final section investigates the subjective perceptions, the meaning of working and the occupational goals of the young adult offspring of foreign workers. As well as sorting out these, at times, contradictory tendencies, the author will try to answer the introductory question: whether it is appropriate to generalize about the social reproduction of an immigrant underclass.

The background and context: status of the foreign worker population

The historical position of the large foreign-worker nationalities in the Federal Republic of Germany differs in a number of ways from that of immigration countries or countries with a colonial legacy. 'Guest'-worker policy has created a system of institutional marginality, which provides a legal basis for the ideology of temporariness. Moreover, the German concept of citizenship and nationality are fundamentally fused.[1] Foreign workers and their offspring do not have a right to citizenship, and the legitimacy of their right to belong to German society continues to be questioned. This has determined perceptions in both the receiving society and amongst the foreign nationalities about the desirability of settlement. Moreover, the bilateral recruitment treaties initiated in the late 1950s and 1960s continue to operate, making former 'guest' workers and their families issues for bargaining between the 'sending' and 'receiving' countries. The significance of this is especially important for the large Turkish community in Germany, but it applies as well to the second largest group, the Yugoslavs. However, since Yugoslavs are generally considered less visible, better educated, more fluent in German and have less children, their special status is less problematic for German society and, as a result, for themselves. That Turkish migrants come from a Muslim culture and are known to adhere to the Islamic religion is an added distinction which mutually reinforces the justification of social distance and drawing social boundaries (Wilpert 1983a).

Thus, in addition to the ideology of temporariness, other factors have led to contradictory policies and a confusion of interests. One confusion is connected with the rights accorded to workers from within the EEC, the other with the role of Turkey in the Western alliance. The first issue means that an EEC migrant has the automatic right to settle and work abroad indefinitely without being forced to give up his original nationality, i.e. to 'assimilate or return'. The second issue means that Turks abroad are an important element in negotiations between Germany and Turkey – whether in the Turkish bid for EEC membership and military aid, or with respect to Germany's representation of the interests of the Western Alliance to guarantee Turkey's loyalty to NATO. Finally, the Turkish government needs and wants to keep the flow of remittances from their citizens abroad. Thus, the Turkish state is also vitally interested that Turks in Germany maintain ties to Turkey.

Owing to the bilateral formalization of the temporariness of migration, the ensuing legal restrictions, and the fixed status of the workers and their families, the decision to stay remains difficult while the transition to settlement is *de facto* in process. Proposals have been made to recognize that the Federal Republic of Germany has become an immigration country for foreign workers and their families. Before the change in 1982 from a Social Democratic to a Conservative government, the political debate was filled with the 'foreign-worker problem' (Wilpert 1983), especially with pleas for integration of the second generation (Kühn 1979) and 'assimilation or return'.

Instead, in the decade since the recruitment of foreign labour was stopped in 1973, new *ad hoc policy* recommendations to further control foreign workers and their family members were repeatedly introduced as well as a one-time voluntary return programme. As will be seen, this general climate has had a significant influence on the future orientations, social distance, and the alternatives perceived by the descendants of foreigners born or raised in Germany. In addition to the ideological distinctions between Germans and foreigners, other factors such as dramatic demographic and cyclical, as well as structural, economic transformations during the last four decades have coloured the general receptiveness to foreigners.

Demographic structure of the foreign and native population
Post-war demography has played an important part in the need to recruit foreign workers in Germany. It was not only the poorly paid, low-ranking, harsh and insecure jobs in the secondary sector of the dual labour market but it was also the lack of skilled manpower in a number of fields that necessitated recruitment outside Germany's borders. Until the building of the Berlin Wall in 1961, a large proportion of the need for skilled and unskilled labour was met by migrants from East Germany.

In addition, there was a particular scarcity of young Germans in the 18- to 25-year-old age group newly entering the labour market. This was due partly to the deficit of births following the Second World War, but it was aggravated by the rising expectations of young Germans, more of whom were taking advantage of the expanding educational system and delaying their entrance into the labour market. In these post-war years, women were also leaving the workforce to bear children.

Signs of change, signalled by the energy crisis, were already apparent in the early seventies. Until the 1973 recruitment stop and entry ban, foreign workers rotated between the countries of origin and the Federal Republic, and except for the 1967 recession year, between 1960 and 1973 more foreign persons departed than enterd Germany annually, averaging about 200,000 yearly (Trommer and Kohler 1981). After 1973 the barriers to entry once returned home contributed to a transformation of the structure of the foreign population and initiated the settlement of workers and their families. This period was marked by the permanent return for some workers and prolonged stays for many others. Between 1974 and 1978 over 400,000 returned yearly. It was also during this phase that the nationality structure of the foreign population shifted. The Spanish population diminished by more than one third, the Greek by one fourth, and the Yugoslav by 10 per cent, the Italians by less than 2 per cent, while the Turkish population with the entry of family members increased by 42 per cent (OECD 1981). In 1985 one-third of all foreigners were of Turkish origin,

Table 5.1   *Demographic structure of Germany in 1984 and foreign population in 1986, according to nationality, per cent*

Age group years	Total population*	Foreign	Turks	Yugoslavs	Italians	Greek	Spanish
0–14	15.5	21.0	30.5	20.0	19.5	19.6	15.1
15–17	4.8	5.0	7.4	3.8	4.5	5.8	4.9
18–20	3.7	5.0	6.6	2.6	5.4	6.0	5.4
21–34	22.9	27.0	22.9	16.4	31.3	21.4	20.8
35–54	14.9	34.2	29.9	49.7	30.05	37.5	40.4
55 and over	28.3	7.8	2.5	6.2	8.4	12.0	13.1
N**	61,175.1	4,512.7	1,434.3	591.2	537.1	278.5	150.5

* includes Germans and foreigners.
** N = thousands
Source: *Statistisches Bundesamt* (1986).

and Turkish youth made up about one-third of all foreign youth (see Table 5.1).[2]

Births of foreign children and family reunions in Germany occurred at a period of imbalance and decline in the demographic structure of the native population. The dense concentration of the foreign population in certain highly industrialized regions and, within these, often in declining inner-city areas, made the presence of foreign, especially of Turkish, youth very visible to local politicians and their constituencies. In certain city districts more children of foreigners than Germans were entering school. In the early eighties, when the German baby boomers reached maturity (18 years) and began to enter the labour market, reactions to the visibility of foreigners were mounting. These parallel events had a direct influence on the scapegoating of foreigners, especially young Turks who were joining their families. Regulations became more restrictive in late 1981 just a few months before the 1982 federal elections. The public debate about the *Ausländerfrage* (the foreigners' issue) then reached its high point.

Policies and regulations

In the years between the 1973 recruitment stop and the 1984 one-time return incentive,[3] a plethora of policy proposals towards foreign workers permeated the political climate. Discussions about integration instead of rotation were accompanied by measures to 'protect' the infrastructure from the high influx of foreigners. The political discussion to promulgate the integration of the second and third generations was offset by a series of restrictions on workers and their family members. A new vocabulary was adopted, 'guest' workers became *Mitbürger* or co-citizens, thus creating the impression of a semblance of recognition as participants in the host society, but without citizenship or electoral rights.

The first restrictive measure enacted after the 1973 recruitment stop was to instruct local employment offices to give priority to Germans in job placement. Foreigners should be hired only when there was no German to fill the job. In the years to follow, political attention was mainly directed at the control of family migration and placing limitations on the entry of the children of workers, such as special restrictions placed on the labour-market entry of the spouses and children joining workers abroad.

Date limits were set in 1974, and once again in 1976, and these limits refused work permits to all children of foreign workers who joined their parents between 1974 and 1979. This practice was changed in April 1979, setting a two-year waiting period before the children of workers newly entering the country could receive a work permit. 'Assimilation or return' became the slogan of the established political Left as well as Right in the run-up to the 1982 federal elections. It was this catchword that made possible the initiative to limit the entry of workers' children over 15 years of age and set new conditions for the admission of the marriage partners of the second-generation offspring of foreign workers living in Germany.

Educational policies

Official policy requires that every foreign child of school age be integrated into a normal class of his/her age level (Kultusminsterkonferenz 1977). Nevertheless, urban housing patterns and school realities have made this impossible. Foreigners live in dense concentrations in certain industrial regions and underprivileged areas of cities. This high geographic focusing of foreigners in certain urban areas resulted in the development of directives to avoid *Uberfremdung* (over-foreignization) of school classes. One of the first educational directives permitted school administrators to establish special classes for foreigners, when the potential share of foreign children in a class surpassed 20 per cent. This exception provided a loophole, which led to the widespread practice of establishing national classes, in most cases for Turkish pupils. A variety of educational policies are permitted by the German system of state control of education. However, policies alone do not necessarily reflect the reality. At every level, discrepancies may be found between official policy and the actual practices put into effect.

The school reality – educational participation and success in school
In 1985, there were slightly over one million foreign children under 16 years of age in the Federal Republic of Germany. These children of school age and younger comprise more than 20 per cent of the total foreign population. About two-thirds of the young foreigners under 15 were born in Germany, as opposed to about 11 per cent of the 15- to 24-year-old age group (*Bundesminister für Arbeit und Sozialordnung* 1986). Owing to the declining birth-rate among the German population, since the 1970s, the share of young foreigners in the educational system will continue to increase in the future.

In 1984/85, there were over 780,000 foreign youngsters in German schools. As a whole, the situation for foreign young people of school age continues to be disadvantageous when compared with their indigenous peers. Between 50 and 60 per cent of foreign pupils complete secondary school with a qualifying certificate, compared to 90 per cent of German school-leavers. Foreign pupils are over-represented in the lowest track of the secondary school system (*Hauptschule*), which is considered to be an educational dead-end. They are, moreover, under-represented in those schools that qualify for academic (*Gymnasium*) or white-collar occupations (*Gymnasium* and *Realschule*). It is this disadvantage in secondary school that also lessens their ability to compete with German youngsters for apprenticeships, since completion of the *Hauptschule* is only a minimal requirement for an apprenticeship.

According to a representative study of the foreign population in 1985 (König *et al.* 1986), over 80 per cent of the 15- to 24-year-old population had attended school in Germany, but only slightly more than half had obtained a school-leaving certificate in 1985. About 40 per cent of these young people (mostly of Turkish origin) had less than five years of schooling in Germany. This was true, however, for about one-third of the other nationalities. If the kind of school-leaving certificate received by those who complete school is examined, there are only slight differences between the nationalities. Most notably, Yugoslav and Greek young people are more likely to have obtained an advanced degree from an occupational school (*Fachoberschule* and *Fachschule*, 25 per cent and 21 per cent, respectively), and Italian and Spanish youth, more often than other nationalities, achieve the university-qualifying degree (the *Abitur*,

8.3 per cent and 10.3 per cent, respectively). This level of attainment remains very low when compared with the native population.

Until now, the presence of foreigners in German schools has contributed to an apparent educational mobility among native pupils. This is well illustrated by data for Berlin schools for the seven-year period between 1979/80 and the 1986/87 academic years (see Table 5.A1). During this time, the number of German pupils in secondary school declined by almost one-quarter (24 per cent), while the number of foreigners grew by one-third. Thus, foreigners comprised 20 per cent of the secondary and one-quarter of the elementary school population in Berlin in 1986. What has been the impact of this change in composition on student participation in the different educational streams? As would be expected, the proportion of foreigners in all types of school has necessarily increased. It has increased least, however, in the academic secondary school (*Gymnasium*), where, at last count (1986), foreigners contributed to about 8 per cent of the student body. However, almost one-half (49.8 per cent) of German young people eligible for secondary school attended this form of school and were able, in the meantime, to increase slightly their likelihood of attendance. Moreover, the *Hauptschule*, already losing its former importance as the normal prerequisite for obtaining apprenticeships, declined the furthest in its absolute numbers of pupils. Once more, it was the German pupils who profited the most. Today, only 8 per cent of German pupils but 35 per cent of the Turks in secondary school in Berlin are likely to attend the *Hauptschule*.

In the 1986/1987 academic year, foreign youngsters totalled 40 per cent of pupils in this least-favoured type of school. Because of the general decline in the German school-age population, the probability of foreigners attending the *Hauptschule* was also reduced. As a result, foreigners more than doubled their share in the comprehensive *Gesamtschule*. Today, about one-third of the foreign school youngsters attend the *Gesamtschule*. Some might argue, however, that this school with its internal streaming is, in reality, replacing the function of the *Hauptschule* in a society where the importance of educational certificates may have become inflated, even though they remain the *sine qua non* for entry into prestigious occupations. There is some evidence to verify this. Currently about one-third of the foreign youngsters leave the *Hauptschule* without a qualifying certificate. In the comprehensive *Gesamtschule*, however, at most about one-half of the children who enrol complete the middle-school certificate, and this is much less for foreigners (14 per cent). In fact, 30 per cent of foreign pupils attending this type of school left in 1986 without a qualifying school-leaving certificate; of the rest, slightly more than half (56 per cent) received their basic *Hauptschule* certificate. In Berlin,

Table 5.2   *School attendance of the 15- to 24-year-old foreigners in Germany in 1985, according to nationality and completion of school certificate, per cent*

	Turks	Yugoslavs	Italians	Greeks	Spanish	Total
Special schools	1.1	1.3	1.7	0.6	2.2	1.3
Grundschule (elementary)	16.4	17.4	22.5	18.2	20.0	17.9
Hauptschule (lower secondary)	41.5	31.3	36.4	30.4	34.4	38.0
Realschule (middle school)	4.8	8.7	7.2	9.4	6.7	6.4
Gymnasium (academic secondary)	2.6	4.3	5.8	6.1	7.8	3.9
Gesamtschule (comprehensive school)	1.3	0.9	2.0	2.8	1.1	1.4
Berufsschule (vocational school)	22.3	24.8	13.9	17.1	20.0	20.5
Fachschule (advanced occupational)	3.4	6.5	3.8	4.4	4.4	4.0
University	1.0	1.7	3.5	6.1	2.2	2.0
Total	100.0	100.0	100.0	100.0	100.0	100.0
Percentage who completed with certificate	41.8	60.2	66.1	66.76	66.0	51.3

Type of school leaving certificates acquired

	Turks	Yugoslavs	Italians	Greeks	Spanish	Total
Special schools	1.7	1.9	1.9	1.1	2.6	1.7
Hauptschule	54.7	47.6	59.6	50.0	53.8	54.2
Realschule	14.5	14.3	18.6	21.3	20.5	16.5
Fachschule	13.4	25.7	9.6	21.3	12.8	15.4
Abitur (academic secondary)	2.8	2.9	8.3	2.1	10.3	4.1
University degree	0.3	0.0	1.3	0.0	0.0	0.4
Other degrees	12.6	7.6	0.6	4.3	0.0	7.7
Total	100.0	100.0	100.0	100.0	100.0	100.0

Source: König *et al.* (1986), 50–53.

Table 5.3   Distribution of German and foreign pupils in Berlin according to type of secondary school attendance in 1979/80 and in 1986/1987, per cent

	Germans		Foreigners		Turks*
	1979	1986	1979	1986	1986
Hauptschulen (first cycle/lower secondary)	13.7	8.0	51.9	26.4	34.9
Realschulen (first cycle/secondary middle school	10.2	16.7	12.0	17.1	16.0
Gesamtschulen (first cycle/secondary – comprehensive	27.6	25.3	18.4	33.6	32.5
Gymnasium (first and second cycle/ secondary – academic	48.3	49.8	17.6	22.7	16.5
	100	100	100	100	100
N =	100,378	75,525	10,296	14,948	9,197

*There is no breakdown available for Turks in 1979/1980 academic year.
Source: Senator für Schulwesen (1987). Author's calculations

for this type of school, these percentages were 13 per cent and 37 per cent on average (Senator für Schulwesen 1987).

The transition to work: labour market participation and the occupational status of the 15- to 25-year-old foreigners

Transformations in the labour market and occupational change
In general, foreign workers of the first generation entered the German labour market at the lowest occupational level, despite higher occupational skills recognized by their home country. The major exception to this are Yugoslav men, well over one-half of whom were employed as skilled workers upon arrival in Germany in 1968. At that time, Turkish men, with 16 per cent in skilled positions, were the second most qualified among the foreign-worker nationalities. More than 95 per cent of all foreigners were employed in manual occupations. This positioning of the majority of the

Table 5.4 Labour market balance sheet for the period from 1970 to 1983: the rate of change in economic activity with respect to the previous year, per cent

Annual average	Economically actives			Self-employed and family helpers			Dependent workers/employees			Registered unemployed		
	Total	Germans	Foreigners	Total	Germans	Foreigners	Total	Germans	Foreigners	Total	Germans	Foreigners
1970	+1.3	−0.5	+31.4	−4.0	−4.1	+6.3	+2.4	+0.4	+32.3	−16.8	−18.2	+66.7
1971	+0.6	−0.7	+17.5	−4.8	−4.9	+9.8	+1.7	+0.3	+17.8	+24.2	+20.1	+140.0
1972	−0.2	−0.9	+7.4	−2.4	−2.5	+8.9	+0.2	−0.6	+7.4	+33.0	+32.4	+41.7
1973	+0.7	−0.1	+9.3	−2.3	−2.5	+8.2	+1.3	+0.3	+9.3	+11.0	+10.5	+17.6
1974	−1.3	−1.0	−4.3	−2.3	−2.5	+9.1	−1.1	−0.7	−4.7	+113.2	+102.8	+245.0
1975	−2.8	−1.8	−13.1	−3.3	−3.3	−1.4	−2.8	−1.5	−13.4	+84.5	+79.9	+118.8
1976	−0.8	−0.4	−6.0	−3.8	−4.1	+11.3	−0.3	+0.3	−6.6	−1.3	+3.4	−29.8
1977	−0.2	+0.0	−2.4	−3.7	−3.9	+6.3	+0.4	+0.7	−2.8	−2.8	−2.3	−7.5
1978	+0.6	+0.7	−0.5	−2.4	−2.6	+7.1	+1.1	+1.3	−0.8	−3.6	−4.6	+6.1
1979	+1.3	+1.1	+3.9	−1.6	−1.9	+8.9	+1.8	+1.6	+3.6	−11.8	−11.9	−10.6
1980	+0.9	+0.6	+4.7	−1.9	−2.0	+2.0	+1.3	+1.0	+4.9	−1.5	−0.1	+15.1
1981*	−0.7	−0.4	−4.9	−2.1	−2.3	+2.0	−0.5	−0.1	−5.3	+43.1	+41.2	+57.0
1982*	−1.9	−1.6	−5.5	−1.8	−1.9	+2.0	−1.9	−1.6	−5.9	+44.1	+43.8	+46.4
1983*	−1.8	—	—	−1.7	—	—	−1.8	—	—	+25.5	+26.0	+22.0

*Estimates.

Source: adapted from *Autorengemeinschaft* (1983), 9.

recruited foreigners has been termed *Unterschichtung*, indicating the substratification of the occupational hierarchy, which permitted natives upward mobility (Hoffmann-Nowotny 1973). In order to gain a wider picture of entry into the labour market by young foreigners, two sets of data available on a national level will be analyzed. The first set covers certain indicators of labour-market participation, branches and economic activity rates, qualifications and unemployment data for the current (1985) 15- to 24-year-old age group, and the situation for the same age group a decade or more earlier from the generation preceding them.

Obviously, this cannot be considered a genuine mobility study, since it was not possible to measure the occupational position of parents and children at the same point in the life-cycle. Instead, it is assumed that 15- to 25-year-olds in 1985 are the children of foreign workers, because the eldest of them would have been 13 years of age at the time of the entry stop (1973). As a whole, the only foreigners who have had access to the labour market since entry stop are the children of workers.

At the height of the recruitment and the year of entry stop, foreign labour accounted for over 10 per cent of the industrial work force in Germany, and as much as one-quarter of the manual labour supply. Even today, foreigners comprise one-third or more of the people filling certain occupational categories in industry (ANBA 1986 b and c).[4]

For our purposes, two labour-market trends, which influence the situation of foreigners and youth, are of special importance since the halt in recruitment. The first trend is the growth and structure of unemployment, and the second is the absolute decline in the size of the labour force. Table 5.4 illustrates the continuous growth of registered unemployed since 1970, peaking in 1974 and levelling off in 1976. In the first phase to 1974, unemployment grew parallel with an increase in the recruitment of foreign labour. In the second phase to 1979, the unemployment of foreigners and natives levelled off, while there was a very slight increase in the size of the native labour force with an annual average of about 1 per cent (Table 5.4).

Since 1980 the absolute number of people employed in Germany has decreased steadily. According to Therborn (1986), Germany is the only Western economy with this trend. This decline has been strongest in manufacturing and among manual workers. Foreigners bore the brunt of redundancies among the industrial labour force between 1974 and 1982. As Table 5.5 illustrates, this is especially noticeable for the periods 1974–77 and 1980–82. In the first phase, foreigners comprised almost half the total number of redundancies

Table 5.5 *The share of foreign workers on employment changes between 1974 and 1982*

Period	Total workers (thousands)	Foreign workers (thousands)	Change in employment accounted for by foreign workers (per cent)
June 1974 – June 1977	− 934.6	− 442.6	47.4
June 1977 – June 1980	+ 1,074.0	+ 183.1	17.1
June 1980 – June 1982	− 482.4	− 262.7	54.5

Source: *Statistisches Bundesamt, Fachserie* 1, *Reihe* 4.2, *Sozialversicherungspflichtige beschäftigte Arbeitnehmer,* yearly (quoted from Dohse (1983) 33.

and in the third phase somewhat more than half. This pattern has also been mirrored in the migration flows and negative balance among employed migrants during this period (Kühl 1987).

Since 1980, the absolute number of people under 20 years of age has declined by almost one-quarter, and the absolute number of foreigners in the work force has decreased by about one-fifth (*Bundesanstalt für Arbeit* 1986b). This means that foreigners were most subject to layoffs, owing to the decline in jobs, and the change in the occupational structure. Moreover, young people under 20 found it increasingly difficult to enter the labour force in this phase. The only segment of the working population that has steadily grown in number is women (German women) and the part-time employed (mainly women) (*Bundesanstalt für Arbeit* 1986c). Contrary to this general trend foreign women lost their share of jobs in the economy. Between 1977 and 1985, more than one-third of the redundancies in manufacturing among women were foreign women. Today, foreign women make up a little more than 10 per cent of the labour force in this sector, in 1977, they totalled about 14 per cent. Although they suffered most from reductions, almost half (42 per cent) being in textiles, foreign women remain over-represented in the harshest and the least attractive branches of industry, such as foundaries, steel, plastics, electronics, and paper.

The service sector accrued the greatest number of jobs in this period. Women, with a 27 per cent increase in the number of jobs, profited slightly more from this expansion than men, whose participation in the service sector grew by 24 per cent. The labour force participation rate of women in Germany still remains, however, behind that of many European countries. None the less, by contrast, the share of foreign women employed in services diminished by 1.2 per cent. The only area where their numbers increased was in cleaning and personal services. This tendency indicates the very different role which foreign and German women continue to play in the labour market. Foreign women tend to enter the manual segment of the service sector and German women the white collar positions in banking and other such services (*Bundesanstalt für Arbeit* 1986c) (see Table 5.6).

Since these trends are based on official data for the dependent labour force, who are required to be socially insured, there remain a certain number of unknowns. It is generally believed that illegal employment has grown especially. Official data do not necessarily reflect the entire spectrum of growth in part-time employment (less than 19 hours weekly). It is likely that many more women, and especially foreigners, are working than are officially registered. Nevertheless, even if the absolute number of foreign women employed part-time, had augmented during this period, pushing them out of the social security system in this way would be a sign of downward mobility. Foreign women and the young have been pushed into the flexible reserve.

Compared to the first generation, not only are young foreigners (15 to 25 year olds) less likely to be economically active today than their age counterparts a decade or more ago, but indicators are that their position within the national economy will differ from that of their parents. In 1986, 54 per cent of foreigners as opposed to 34 per cent of natives were employed in manufacturing. This was about 25 per cent fewer foreigners in manufacturing than a decade before (*Bundesanstalt für Arbeit* 1986b).

A more exact indicator of the occupational position of young foreigners can be ascertained by looking at their occupational skills (see Table 5.A2). According to the federal labour office (*Bundesanstalt für Arbeit* 1987b), about 64 per cent of 15- to 20-year-old Germans and 88 per cent of the respective foreigners who are economically active were employed as workers. As illustrated in Table 5.A2, whilst 10 per cent of the German young people between 15 and 19 years old were skilled, this was true for only 4 per cent of foreigners. It is even more revealing to look at the next age group (20 to 24 years), where educational training is normally completed. In this age group, half of the German young people holding jobs are employed as workers, and about half of these are skilled. However

Table 5.6 *Sectoral change in employment among the socially insured employed between 1976 and 1986, according to nationality (1976 = 100) and share of employed in 1986 according to sector*

| | Total population | | Foreigners | |
	Number	Per cent	Number	Per cent
Agriculture, forestry, fishing	234,203	+19.3	14,064	−25.2
Energy, mining	477,133	−4.4	33,348	−21.5
Manufacturing	8,300,392	−1.6	865,560	−24.7
Construction	1,496,609	−15.0	145,854	−29.1
Commerce	2,829,921	+2.1	102,761	−2.2
Transport, communications	1,016,937	+5.0	60,936	−16.1
Banking, insurance	846,034	+17.0	12,804	+4.4
Services, unless otherwise mentioned	4,095,874	+34.3	293,548	+9.8
Non-profit organizations	454,172	+39.7	17,132	+42.0
Territorial bodies, social insurance	1,441,274	+9.2	46,994	−3.6
Total			1,600,216	−17.4

Source: *Bundesanstalt für Arbeit* (1986b).

almost 90 per cent of foreign young people continue to be manual labourers and fewer than 20 per cent of these are skilled.

Youth unemployment
Young foreigners are coming of age and entering the working world in a period characterized by turbulent transformations in the structure of employment, and the declining participation of youth in the economy. In fact, it is a time when the future of work and occupations are generally unpredictable. To combat the signs of unemployment, the federal government has developed a series of special programmes, which included extending the number of years of compulsory schooling to ten years and by supporting the expansion of occupational training courses outside the labour market (*überbetrieblich Massnahmen*) (Schober 1986). Thus, although the absolute number of young people employed has declined by 24 per

cent since 1980 (ANBA 1986), the official unemployment rate of youth remains relatively low. In 1985, when the average rate of unemployment was 10 per cent, the official unemployment rate for youth under 20 years of age was 8.1 per cent. Foreign youths in this age group were, however, twice as likely as natives to be registered as unemployed. Increasingly, programmes for young people in the 15- to 20-year-old age group have caused the delay in real unemployment to the 20- to 25-year-old age group, who, in 1985, were 17 per cent of the overall number of unemployed (Schober 1986). The official figures on unemployment camouflage the real extent of unemployment among young people of foreign origin. This is due to the restrictive definition of unemployment. For statistical purposes, the unemployed are only those people who register as unemployed since they are eligible to draw benefits. Very few young persons under 20 years of age fall into this category, since to become eligible for unemployment previous employment is required. Unemployment among youth is estimated to be at least as twice as high as officially registered. And, this would be even higher for foreign youth. Because of their legal status foreigners are frequently insecure about registering for unemployment or other benefits for fear of jeopardizing their permit to stay. However, a closer look at the Berlin situation where more precise data is available indicates that foreign people under 20 years of age represented more than one quarter of the unemployed in this age group (that is, almost four times their share of the population). (*Landesarbeitsamt Berlin* 1986). Attempts to reconstruct the whereabouts of the foreign and native youths between the ages of 15 and 24 years is difficult because of the diverse statistical breakdowns used by the *Statistisches Bundesamt* and the *Bundesanstalt für Arbeit*. Foreign young persons are estimated, however, to be more than three times as likely to be unemployed as natives. If they are involved in education and training programmes, they are over-represented in programmes that offer little competitive value for skilled or more qualified occupational careers (*Bundesminister für Bildung*, 1986).

Occupational training
Attendance of the occupational school (*Berufsschle*) is mandatory until the age of 18. However, certification as a skilled worker is only possible if an apprenticeship is obtained at the same time. According to the latest report of the federal Minister of Education, there were 204,000 foreign youths in the 15- to 18-year-old age group in 1984. More than one-third (37 per cent) of the young people in this age group were not receiving any form of educational or occupational training (*Bundesminister für Bildung* 1986). During

the 1984/85 academic year, about one-quarter of foreign young people (18 per cent of Turks) in the 15- to 18-year-old age group were in training as apprentices in the dual system. About 10 per cent (5 per cent of Turks) participated in academic or full-time occupational training programmes. This would mean that at most about one-third of foreign youth were participating in programmes that further their qualifications and may provide a basis for occupational mobility.

It is necessary to be aware, that even these figures are relatively optimistic, since almost one-quarter of participants in apprenticeships are generally dropped or drop out before completion. Also, only about one-half of those who complete training are hired in their field. The rest enter other fields, usually dequalified, or become unemployed (13 per cent) (Schober 1986). These general trends are heightened for foreigners, since they tend to enter the apprenticeships that produce an over-supply for the labour market and are most subject to unemployment.

A longitudinal comparative study of 1977 school-leavers demonstrates the relative disadvantage of foreign youth, even when they have the same basic qualifications as their German peers (Stegmann 1981). Three years after completing school successfully, about 20 per cent of foreigners as compared with 11 per cent of Germans were not involved in some form of occupational training. More than 75 per cent of young men of foreign origin were in vocational training programmes for manual labourers in industry; this was true for only a little more than half (57 per cent) of German males. For both nationalities, the girls were more disadvantaged. Federal data on apprenticeships according to nationality indicate that this trend in occupational training is now even more pronounced than it was in 1980. Whilst more than 75 per cent of foreign young people who had an apprenticeship obtained it in a manual occupation, this was true for about one-half of Germans (53.6 per cent). This inequality in opportunities extends to the types of apprenticeships as well. Almost one-half of German young people have apprenticeships in white-collar professions, which is true for about one-quarter of the foreign young people in training (*Bundesanstalt für Arbeit* 1987b). Those who have completed school successfully in Germany are clearly more likely also to complete training. Also, young women, even though they are generally more successful in school, remain disadvantaged with respect to occupational training. Young women are more likely to train in occupations that over-produce for the labour market, thus increasing their vulnerability for unemployment, even after completion of training. Federal data reveals that 60 per cent of all foreign women who are receiving any training at all are being taught in one of three occupational areas: hairdressing, health services and commerce (*Bundesminister für Bildung* 1986: 92).

Special programmes – pre-vocational training

The most extensive special programme conceived to prepare foreign youth for entry into the labour market is the MBSE for pre-vocational and social training. It was originally directed towards youth who entered Germany late in adolescence and was made conditional for receiving a work permit. The waiting-period regulations required foreign youth to attend a ten-month occupational preparatory course, which comprised language instruction, general education and social orientation, and a broad introduction into three occupational areas.

Serving as a socialization agent, giving the unemployed some hope and otherwise keeping those with no other possibilities off the street, the MBSE programme aided a little more than one-third of all participants to find a job (24 per cent) or an apprenticeship (13 per cent) upon completion in 1984 (*Bundesminister für Bildung* 1986). Since then, this programme has dwindled in size and significance and the pre-vocational training of foreign youngsters is being serviced by other programmes available to unemployed young people.

Some preliminary conclusions about the transition to work

The foregoing analysis from data on education, training, and occupational status of the first wave of descendants of foreign workers leads to some tentative conclusions. Demographic and labour market conditions have led to increased competition with natives of the same age group. The current position of the second generation may be characterized as not only disadvantageous with respect to their German peers, but also generally inferior to that of the first generation of this age group at their initial arrival. Exceptions may be found only among the small minority of foreign youth who secure viable apprenticeships or who enter into higher education.

If the first generation is taken as an example, it becomes evident that, the labour-market situation of foreigners in the German economy is not homogeneous. As the above analysis demonstrates, young foreigners, as their parents, might be very roughly classified into one of three groups (Dohse 1983):

- A group who has found a stable position in the economy. Among the parents this is exemplified by their longevity in one firm. They have weathered the storm of two recessions and will most likely continue to do so.

- A group with unstable employment fluctuating in and out of work.
- Those working in the jobs of the invisible economy.

Although these observations were made about the first generation, with some variations it comes close to the situation of the young adult descendants of foreigners. It, too, offers some disturbing implications about the impact of this situation on the future status of the second generation. Among the descendants of foreigners, those in the first group are the minority who have found a viable future-oriented apprenticeship. Obviously, the distinction made between the second and third above categories is more analytical than real. It is very likely that the same individuals may enter in and out of both types of job markets. Nevertheless, the third category is an economic loophole, which is particularly attractive to the most vulnerable members of the foreign population. They resort to this illegal market because of the restrictions on work permits for spouses and children of workers joining their families. Also the small number of current second generation who have been able to obtain apprenticeships with a viable future, in hard times, makes them candidates as well for jobs in both the second and third category. How do these objective conditions match the subjective aspirations of the second generation? How likely are they to hold the same instrumental attitude towards work in the German economy as their parents? Are there any factors that would indicate their susceptibility to replacing the function of their parents in the lower segment of the dual labour market?

Work values, community formation and the location of reference groups[5]

The migration venture: values and alternatives of the first generation

> Germans are not like us. The Germans work the whole day, but in the evening they go out where they can forget their problems. They're not very happy with their life either. After all Germans are forced to work here; that's not the case for me. If I want, if I don't like it here anymore, than I can go back to my country. Of course, Germans are not forced to save money. Whatever they earn they spend, whereas some of us Turks feel forced to save. But, then we don't live like human beings. (A 40-year-old first-generation Turkish construction worker, who had lived in Berlin 16 years at the time of the interview).

Since a special attitude towards work is essential to international labour migration, it is also central to an understanding of the transition from one generation to the next. The work-values of first-generation immigrant workers are primarily instrumental. The motivation to work abroad is characterized by its conditioned temporariness to improve a person's lot and to achieve social recognition in the country of origin. The community of reference is the community of origin. This is the *sine qua non* of international labour migration which all first-generation migrants share. As an outsider he or she is temporarily willing to perform tasks recognized as low ranking, outside of his own community. In this section, there are several questions to investigate: (a) what has been the influence of international migration on the descendants of migrants? (Whether the second generation holds the same instrumental attitude towards work as their parents?); (b) does the emergence of a second generation socialized in the new country eliminate the possibility of adopting an attitude of temporary accommodation to an inferior position within their society of residence; and (c) what is the role of the community in formation, who are the reference groups that satisfy social recognition?

The socialization context: family goals and the aspirations of parents and children

The instrumental work values of parents for social betterment at home upon return are paralleled by aspirations for social mobility for their children. The goals of the migration venture are family goals:

> My parents came here to earn some money, to prepare a good future for us. They've done more than they planned. It would not have been possible to do more. They have bought much in the home country. Everything is prepared, they could return now if they want... When I finish my studies, then I won't stay here one more day. I don't like Germany. Actually I would like to return immediately, but I would have no chance to study in Turkey. If I wouldn't have come here at all, then maybe I would have gotten some education there. (A 17-year-old Turkish boy who has lived in Berlin since he was eight, who is preparing to transfer from the *Realschule* (middle school) to the *Gymnasium* (academic secondary)

The narrative interviews of parents as well as children give high priority to self-direction and becoming one's own boss. They repeatedly express the hope of avoiding the subjugating work of the 'guest' worker. This boy's parents aspire that their son will one day have it better than they have had, as his mother puts it:

> If the boy studies, then he can stay here, but I also want him to eventually return. It's better for him to be his own boss in Turkey, than to become a worker here. It's very tough to be a worker.

Migration has been a family venture. In some families, aspirations for children have been high: as another Turkish mother of two children explains, her work is to help her husband guarantee the education of their children. If her son can go to the university, she will not return to Turkey, since their goals will have been acheived:

> We came from our village to Istanbul. In order to help my husband I worked in a factory... When I saw that the situation was worsening, I told my husband that I would go to Germany and send for him later. My husband had nothing against it... I was quickly accepted. I went with my sister to West Germany... We came here to secure our income, but had no idea how long we were going to stay at that time... I left my six year old child there... But after a while I couldn't stand it any longer, and I sent for my son. I thought that he would get a better education here... He should go to school as long as he wants,... Once the children speak German very well, they can go to the university. If he goes to the university, then I will stop working and stay home, and only his father will work.

For this working mother as in many other families, there are two possible ways of securing the future. One is for both parents to work, saving and investing for return. The other is through the education of their children. Education is highly valued in Turkey, and prolonged schooling should transfer into occupational opportunities and social mobility. As a whole, the majority of children desire a better occupation than that of their parents.

It has been found that the children of foreign workers adhere to success goals as much, or more so, than their German peers (Wilpert 1980), and that these high aspirations are integrally related to the phenomenon of labour migration. The involvement of parents in dirty, intensive, and alienating working conditions was considered a temporary condition in order to avoid the same status for the next generation. In this case, it is not necessarily settlement and the change of reference groups that have raised the aspirations of the second generation, but rather family goals and aspirations for a better future forged in the migration venture. Educational and occupational aspirations are found to be high, for example in the case of Turkish youngsters, even when they attend segregated classes and have little contact with German pupils.

Such an observation leads some to argue that these aspirations are maladaptive, or that, since parents see education as primarily instrumental to social mobility, they do not understand or support the content and underlying values of education. Interpreted as holding unrealistic goals, these youth are considered not properly socialized to working class conditions.[6] According to this line of thought, the social reproduction of migrants to the working class is taken for granted. What does it mean to be socialized to working class conditions? Does it mean the search for security, a stable job and a steady income, as Piore (1979) suggests? Or, does being a member of the working class mean that a person forfeits his or her individual aspirations for social mobility? What is the significance of these occupational aspirations once young people are confronted with the reality of the labour market?

Aspirations and work values of the 16 year old and older school leavers

After I left school, I wanted to become an accountant... I wanted to find an apprenticeship. I was tested in a firm, and they sent me an invitation. 'You passed the test, come for an interview.' I really thought that I was already accepted. I went and after talking a while they told me they didn't have a position now, but when one was free they would take me. If I wanted I could begin now as a worker, but for the wage of an apprentice. I didn't agree to that... I attended a couple of courses, but it came to nothing. They didn't take me anywhere. They had no openings for apprentices, that's why I was forced to become a worker. I couldn't become anything better than a worker. (An 18-year-old semi-skilled carpenter who arrived in Berlin at eight years of age.)

Studies that focus on the occupational aspirations of secondary school-leavers shed light on some of these issues. These youth are in a phase in the life-cycle where most decisions about future vocational choice have already been narrowed down because of the type of secondary school they attended, or failed to attend. Information collected by the state employment agency reveals in fact that little difference exists between the occupational aspirations of German and foreign youth in this category (*Bundesminister für Bildung* 1986; Jenschke 1982).

Job security is the most important quality that German and foreign youth alike seek when choosing their future occupation. In fact, a longitudinal study of *Hauptschul* school-leavers also observes that the parents of foreign youth are more likely to have a more realistic orientation towards actual available training and job opportunities than German parents, the latter tending to put greater emphasis on the interests, talents and desires of their children when recommending job preferences. (Stegmann 1981).

Research with a cross-section of Turkish and Yugoslav young people in Berlin schools (Wilpert 1983) would support this. Although foreign youth expressed high occupational and educational goals while in elementary and certain secondary schools, once the opportunities were perceived as limited, after they had left school or entered vocational training programmes, they overwhelmingly indicated a desire to find an apprenticeship and learn a skilled occupation.

The daughters of migrant workers
In an early study among Turk and Yugoslav pupils in Berlin, it

was found that the occupational aspirations of the foreign school-girls were higher than those of their German peers in similar schools (Wilpert 1980). They were also unusually higher than found in the literature about the occupational aspirations of working class girls (Bednarz 1978). The aspirations of these young women are not, however, without contradictions. According to Weische-Alexa (1978), Turkish young women schooled in Germany have concrete occupational goals, experience a certain feeling of freedom in occupational choice, coupled, however, with strong family orientation and less liberty in leisure activities. The ambivalence that these young women experience was also recorded in other research on German young women (Mollwo 1976; Projektgruppe 1977).

Nevertheless, girls who have dropped out of school without a qualifying certificate frequently articulate their disillusionment at being a worker. They expressed dissatisfaction with their current status:

> Besides money, there's nothing to life here. I wasn't even able to finish school here – if I would have stayed in Turkey I would have finished school ... I really didn't want to come here ... What did I turn out to be? Just a factory worker. If I would have stayed in Turkey I would have gotten training, then I could have done something more useful. (A 19-year-old seamstress in textiles, who arrived at nine years of age and dropped out of school at 17.)

> I'd like to work, but not behind the machine ... I don't want to work on a machine. I know – my mother doesn't like it either. (But) my mother didn't go to school, she wasn't allowed to. She does it (works on machines) because she has to. (A 16-year-old female school-leaver, who arrived in Berlin at five years of age.)

It has also been their disillusionment at not finding an apprenticeship in the field they desired, or negative experiences with the occupational schools, which has caused some girls to give up their original aspirations and enter immediately into the labour market. Finding a good apprenticeship, for example in a doctor's office, is difficult. The waiting lists for entry into attractive professions – kindergarten teaching, nursing, and so on – are long, and selection is highly competitive. Moreover, apprenticeships require an investment of two to three years before they are completed. The pay during this period is about one-third the normal wage. At times, this has been incompatible with the return orientation of the family. Attendance at vocational training school without hope of an apprenticeship is detrimental to securing work, and offers no recognized certificate for better future status. 'They teach nothing.' 'We learn something about housekeeping, but since it's only one day a week, you don't learn anything. It's of no value.' These are the remarks of young women who thought that education in Germany might lead to a better future. Opportunities to realize goals are limited. Early entrance into the labour market or even marriage may appear to be the most viable alternatives. By pursuing the educational and occupational histories of some of the young people involved in earlier studies (Wilpert 1980, 1982), it has been possible to observe the impact that the phase in the life-cycle has on the modes of adaptation and strategies developed by young women and men entering adulthood.

For example, after an experience in the working world, or not being satisfied with the hopefully desired liberating effects of marriage, some young women, who dropped out of school, develop new strategies to supplement their education and open up new alternatives so they can leave their dead-end-jobs.

Personal autonomy on the job, its potential for advancement, and the use of the occupation in Turkey are all values that retain importance among these young women, despite barriers they have experienced to their original goals. They, too, give high priority to self-direction and being one's own boss:

> Now I am cleaning in a firm where my mother works... I plan to continue until I can get accepted in the Arts school... I didn't want a normal job. I didn't want to work in a factory. It's even stricter there. You always have to be there at the same time. You leave at the same time. The *Meister* (boss) is always at your side, and so on. Even though you can earn more in a factory, I didn't want to work there. The pay is higher, but I am satisfied enough with cleaning, since no one controls me. The work is my own work! (A 19-year-old woman, who dropped out of the *Gymnasium*, who now works in cleaning, but strives to enter the school of arts)

The dominant theme among many young women who are employed as workers is that their current work is transitional. They are interested in good working conditions, training for advancement, and setting future goals beyond their current status and the work of their mothers. Major generational differences are observable between first-generation immigrants and their daughters with respect to the motivation to work and to continue their education and training. In the mothers' case, even when they took the initiative in migration, their motivation to work was linked primarily to family goals to promote the future social position and security of the family and children. The attitudes of the daughters of first-generation foreign women are more oriented towards individual goals and personal autonomy than was possible for their mothers.

At the same time, it is necessary to differentiate the women as well as the men among the descendants of foreign workers. Family backgrounds, migration patterns and cultural resources must all be considered. Cultural differences in problem-solving strategies may be expected when young women experience discrepancies between aspirations and opportunities. The cultural expectations and the social resources available to develop new strategies vary. Young women from different cultural backgrounds also see different alternatives for solving the blocked opportunities they confront. Given a lack of training opportunities, some young foreign women may choose to work in low-skilled occupations instead of attending the vocational training school. Work provides a needed income for the unknown, but desired, future of the whole family. Their economic status as workers may bring recognition and a certain amount of bargaining power. For many women, however, marriage is the cultural norm. It is through marriage, settling down and having a family that a person enters into adulthood. Only higher education, which promises access to professional life, is an acceptable alternative – in fact, a prestigious reason for delaying marriage. To understand better the various strategies young women as well as young men develop, it is necessary to look at the community in formation and the alternatives that diverse family backgrounds provide. Beforehand, however, it might be useful to attempt to summarize briefly the work attitudes found among the descendants of migrants.

Work value patterns and identification
Autonomy, advancement and future security are the values Turkish young people of both sexes seek in work and occupations. Being a school drop-out does not always dampen these long-range aspirations. Nevertheless, the lives and choices these young people make indicate something as well about resources and constraints rooted in social and cultural origins. Identificational factors, too, play a role in shaping the strategies they develop. Five general tendencies in work-related values emerge, and these might be roughly grouped in the following way:

Work in Germany is instrumental   Work is a job that secures survival now and guarantees a future for the family. The work they have found may not be the work that they have sought, but it provides the hope of relative job security. These young people between 18 and 24 are married and have taken on adult responsibilities. In view of widespread unemployment, and lacking the outlook for similar opportunities in the area of origin, young adults in this category appear to have come to terms with their future as workers in Germany. They are happy to have a job.

Work in Germany is temporary Work is instrumental to ensure return. At least two sub-types of young people may be found in this category. One sub-type boasts a strategy similar to that of their parents; to work three or four years, earn some money, and then return to open up a shop or to drive a taxi;

> I want to have decent work, three or four years of real work and then return to Turkey . . . Anykind. Just work. Where one can earn a lot of money. (An unemployed 18 year old who had lived in Germany five years at the time of the interview)

Another sub-type added the dimension to learn and earn for return:

> But I won't return until I have attended some courses and learnt an occupation, even if it should be difficult. Once I am certain that I can have a job in Turkey then I will return.

They seek a certified qualification in order to establish themselves, very often in the small business that their parents once strove for. Financed with the family savings, they hope to set up a shop as a hairdresser, electrician, plumber, car mechanic, or a TV technician.

Work as a manual labourer is temporary It is instrumental, but a step along a lengthy path towards occupational qualifications and social mobility. The future is open, alternatives are perceived, and there are steps to be taken:

> I wasn't able to get the apprenticeship of my choice. My brother organized my current job. When he was finished, I took his place as a mechanic . . . After I finish, if I manage, I want to continue to go to school. I would like to become an engineer . . . That is, if I can complete my journeyman's test. Then I would work two years to become a *Meister*. It would take all in all about five to seven years. (A 19-year-old apprentice who arrived in Berlin at four years of age)

For young women, it is through a profession that is socially recognized that they can imagine negotiating a little bit of space in their lives. To achieve this, many young women follow courses, to earn the High School diploma, German courses to help them move from the factory belt to sales or enter the offices through secretarial training. For many young Turkish women who still foresee a later future in Turkey, work and a bit of autonomy and social recognition in their lives are only possible through a white-collar occupation.

Work as career To allow for greater flexibility, the ideal career is useful as a future occupation in two cultures. Young people who have been educationally successful, or who still hope to achieve educational success, desire an occupation that may be adaptable to two countries, and so form a bridge between cultures.

The interface between work values and return orientations

For first-generation migrants, the return orientation, or the 'myth' of return, gives purpose to the hard lives led in a foreign environment. For their offspring, raised and socialized in their country of work, it is not a foreign environment; in many cases, it is less foreign than that which they would (or do) find in their parents' place of origin. Despite this, the return orientation continues to persist for a number of young people. One explanation for this is that it is a means of adapting to the anomic conditions, the discrepancy experienced between personal goals and the means to achieve these (Hoffmann-Nowotny 1973; Wilpert 1980) – a way to come to terms with the failure of the migration venture.

Two major variables appear to play a significant role here, and these can be tested only over time and through comparative country studies. There exists, for all second-generation Turks, a tension between their lack of a legitimate future and membership of German society (institutional marginality) and the *de facto* experience of a legitimate claim to belongingness through a life lived (via secondary socialization, participation in school, work, culture and mass society). This experience may be somewhat parallel to the perception of a legitimate claim to self-determination accrued in the principle of territoriality. This conflict is enhanced by the ascriptive experiences of discrimination, denigration and youths' concomittant identification with their family and culture of origin. Life in two societies offers positive as well as negative elements; each may, at times, be a welcome alternative.

The point is not, however, that there will be massive returns of young people but rather that the return of orientation to be found among young foreigners in Germany is related to their impossibility to identify with a future in that country. Those who do find it possible belong either to the few who perceive relative opportunities or, to those who, because of their previous experience as a denigrated minority in their country of origin, view the alternatives in Germany as no worse and possibly materially better.

Thus, despite the rather high aspirations observed among the offspring of Turkish migrants, different attitudes develop about work and the job each finds. In this sense, work-values may develop and change from original occupational aspirations. Experiences in Germany and a change in expectations may cause acculturation to working class values for some young people; these may be the same young people we find in the first category. Others retain their mobility aspirations either for self-employment, in Germany or the country of origin, the goals of the family venture, or for a profession. What has been found is that the strategies youth develop cannot be solely explained by the classical indicators of socio-economic status. Rather, both family resources (background and migration patterns) as well as experiences in Germany interact to help them form and change their strategies. In many cases, there exists a dissonance between aspirations and opportunities. In addition to background factors, experiences during the settlement process influence the alternatives perceived. To what extent are these young people willing to adapt their aspirations to the alternatives available? Is it possible to speak about the existence of a 'second-generation' community?

Settlement and community formation
As has been seen, despite length of stay in Germany, identification with the country of origin and even the desire to live there in the future remain strong among the descendants of migrants who have attended, or who are still attending, schools in Germany. This return orientation among a certain segment of foreign youth would appear to contradict theories about the influence of settlement on the future orientations of the second generation.

One signficant factor that may help explain this apparent contradiction among young people who have spent more than half their life in Germany is connected with the kind of migrant community that has formed. Piore (1979) speaks about second-generation communities that may take the form of an extension of the area of origin; he calls these settlements without assimilation. Although this typology is an extreme simplification of the social structure of an immigrant community, there are some elements in his analysis that may help contribute to an understanding of the processes that foreign-worker communities are now undergoing in Europe.

Theoretically, settlement and community formation, the establishment of a system of social relations in the country of residence, should involve transferring the reference group from the society of origin of the parents to the society of birth or socialization. There is no doubt that this potential exists, considering the very complex settlement of Turks in Berlin and in numerous other urban areas in the Federal Republic of Germany. Elsewhere, the complexity of the social relations and social organization of Berlin Turks has been reported (Gitmez and Wilpert 1987). Speaking of a community of Turks is not meant to suggest anything like a cohesive, homogeneous, or 'natural' community.

Numerous and extensive ties have been established between settlements of Turks in Germany and Turkey. Turkish institutions and social networks have taken shape in Berlin and other parts of Germany. These represent both an extension and a transformation of social relations, kin and solidarity patterns as known in Turkey. There exist beside one another initiatives to recreate old forms, to reify ideologies, myths and beliefs unresolved in the past, as well as the creation of new forms. There is not one community but several. These forms of socializing among Turks are visible for self and others, but they may also be points of differentiation within the whole 'community'. Until now, it remains a community primarily formed by the first generation. The second generation growing into this community has not yet reached the maturity necessary to influence its shape.

What does this 'community' mean to the second generation? Does it mean that reference groups are transferred? As is reflected in the wide range of occupational aspirations and work-values of young adults, it would seem that this question can not be uniformly answered. To some, Germany is an extension of Turkey, lived through trans-national family ties and village networks operating here and there. For others, it is, above all, a location which symbolizes identification at many different levels, through the presence of Turks coming and going on the streets, in parks, playgrounds and sport fields. Parts of Berlin are thought of as Turkish. It's a migrant's territory, a piece of space where he or she is at home away from 'home'. For Turkish women, certain neighbourhoods are places where a person is being judged and responded to with sets of values operant in traditional Turkish society. For some, it is 'settlement without assimilation'. Turkish society in the homeland is not, however, uniform, cohesive or monocultural. Nor is Turkish society in Germany. Alternatives exist with which a second-generation Turk may identify.

Alternatives available and the location of reference groups
The Turkish population in Germany can be differentiated according to certain characteristics of origin. These may be founded on language, ethnic backgrounds, religious beliefs, conflicting ideologies (ranging from conservative to more secular or fundamentalist), distinct village migration networks, different motivations towards a possible future in Germany, or tolerance towards living as a minority (Gitmez and Wilpert 1987). Another important factor is the great variation to be found in the educational and other resources that

differentiate families, for example their migration patterns, the mother's role in the family, motivations, the extent of fragmentation the family has experienced, which in turn influences the achievement of the children.

Out of a cluster of attributes that combine factors of cultural background with family structure and social resources, a variation in family types, which influence the socialization and education of children, has been identified. So far, it has been found that family background, being a minority in the country of origin, is more important for the openness parents express towards establishing a future in Germany and towards German citizenship for their children than, for example, material values, such as the occupational aspirations parents hold for their children (Wilpert 1987).

When the minority, in the Turkish case a minority within a minority, maintains its old patterns of solidarity and allegiances, transferring them to the next generation, this may be considered 'settlement without assimilation'. For the majority of the second generation, however, it is more likely a question of settlement without identification, as settled outsiders. This has to do with the institutional conditions which, as noted earlier, define foreignness and eligibility for, or desirability of, citizenship. First- and second-generation Turks are forced by their outsider role in German society to assume an umbrella-like corporate identity. In the case of Turks, a Turkish identity, the ideal of Ata Turk and Turkish nationalists not fully realized in the homeland, may be a tenuous identification for first- and second-generation Turks abroad. Certain minorities subsumed under the power of the monocultural and laic Turkish state propose identities to their young in Germany. For example, different degrees of Kurdish consciousness and linguistic fluency have been activated even among the youngest abroad. In a similar way, Islamic organizations and Muslim identity offer an alternative identity to the Turkish one, and some of these are conflicting identities. In addition to these formally organized and publically vocalized programmes addressed to different segments of the Turkish population, there are other minorities, for example, smaller (Circassian) and larger (Alevi) sub-groups who are have been able, through international migration, to rediscover, renew or to reaffirm identities suppressed and forbidden articulation in Turkey. Nevertheless, these 'communities' or social entities still offer distinct cultural resources and family socialization patterns which may remain alternative models for young Turkish foreigners in German society. In some cases, the solidarity patterns expressd within the community may provide a more important source of identity than work; in others, it permits continued identification with the area of origin.

Conclusions

The legal and ideological situation in the Federal Republic of Germany has contributed to the creation of a second generation of foreigners. A 'guest' worker and his family are not potential immigrants, and the response of the descendants of foreign workers is dissatisfaction with the conditions of recruitment and entry applied to their parents. It is the combination of evolved *ad hoc* 'guest' worker policies and transformations on the labour market that mark the situation faced by second-generation foreigners during transition from school to work.

On the whole, the position of young adult offspring of foreigners on the labour market is disadvantageous, not only in relation to German peers, but also when compared with the first generation on their arrival. In other words, ethnic substratification continues for the majority. This is programmed by their limited educational opportunities and poor access to occupational training that holds any promise for the future. Still, substratification is not absolute. The persistence of parents to pursue their initial objectives, the energy invested into the achievement of goals and the future of children will materialize for a minority – for the few who have been able to use family resources and who have met relative opportunities. These opportunities have been created, on the one hand, by their personal resources, and, on the other, by a fortunate combination of circumstances, geographical location, timing of arrival in an area, the quality of the local education system or its community.

Whether or not those of the second generation who experience blocked opportunities will be adaptable and suited to fill the function their parents did within the secondary sector of the dual labour market is not easy to answer. The educational and occupational aspirations of a number of young people in education and training would speak against this. Their future work and occupational objectives stress instead the goals of greater security, autonomy and advancement. These are not necessarily objectives that would prepare them to accept the conditions of the lower segment of the dual labour market on a long-term basis.

A variety of work-related values and strategies have been observed. This is partially explained by the alternatives available, the unknown future of numerous occupations. It is also accounted for by factors of settlement and community formation and the background of the culture of origin intervening, influencing the location of reference groups and the continued effectiveness of cultural norms as well as patterns of identification. These factors impinge on the emerging work-values and future aspirations of these young persons. As has been seen among Turks, there will be a certain group finding and accepting entrance into the stable working class. However, this is currently a real alternative for only a minority. The great majority face unsteady work, a high turnover of jobs, and insecure occupational futures. The fact that a certain number of the current 15- to 24-year-old population retain their homeward orientation might be a determining factor. For some, the plan to return continues and makes it possible to endure what is accepted as temporary, because social recognition is expected among a person's own kin in Turkey. For others, like the Kurdish minority, return for a variety of reasons is not attractive, and being a minority and a worker in Germany may not be the worst of alternatives. For some of these minorities, who have entered Germany as chain migrants, villager and kinship ties may remain important resources that are not necessarily available to isolated migrant families or to the indigeneous population.

The focus of this chapter has been primarily on the descendants of migrant families of Turkish origin, the largest and most discriminiated minority. Nevertheless, a number of observations made about the descendants of Turks would apply to other nationalities as well. Although there does exist a hierarchy of social distance and tolerance in which the Turks rank especially low, other nationalities may also experience an outsider role in German society. Young people of all nationalities share aspirations for a better life, a more secure future, and acceptance of the value of their origins. Differences in achievement, which may be found between nationalities in educational or occupational mobility, are primarily the result of the timing of migration and the educational resources in the family brought from the country of origin. Networks and 'micro-communities' are dense among several other nationalities: for example there are many Italian, Greek or Spanish foreigners in Germany. However, the size and especially the density of these other nationalities are more limited. It is not clear whether their size is offset by the proximity of the countries of origin and the intensity of multiple-communication networks. Similarly, it can not be assumed that any of the foreign-worker populations in Germany or elsewhere are necessarily homogeneous. Internal stratification and diverse patterns of migration and settlement exist, as well. These foreign-worker populations deserve attention, their cultural identity is formed in the interplay between the resources of origin and the life lived abroad.

Until the end of the 1990s, when the forecast for skilled manpower may be more optimistic, because fewer young Germans will be available due to the German birth deficit in the early seventies, the majority of foreign youth will be forced into the flexibile reserve and the invisible economy. This is the logical extension of their permanent temporariness and their reduced opportunities to achieve skilled training, when compared with many of their parents who may have brought their skills with them. These young foreigners do, however, have different ways of dealing with this situation.

Notes

1. The right to German citizenship is based on ethnic origins (*jus sanguinis*, i.e. *deutsche Volkszugehörigkeit*) or stemming from a family which was present within the 31.12.37 boundaries of the German Reich (Fleischer 1983:531). The majority of these people have entered Germany in connection with long-standing negotiations with Rumania, the Soviet Union, Hungary and Poland.

2. The birth-rate among Germans began steadily to decline, the birth-rate among foreign residents grew. In 1974, it was more than three times as high among foreigners per 1,000 inhabitants (26.7) than among Germans (8.8) (Trommer and Kohler 1981, p. 180). That year, the number of live births of foreign children comprised 17.4 per cent of total births in the Federal Republic of Germany, at a period when the foreign population was 10 per cent. In recent years, when foreigners contribute to around 7 per cent of the total population, births among foreigners have declined to less than 12 per cent annually (Beauftragte der Bundesregierung 1986).

3. The federal government sponsored a one-off repatriation scheme between October 1983 and September 1984. Some 189,000 Turks were reported to have left the country during this time. This policy applied only to foreign workers from non-EEC countries. The regulation waived as well the normal two-year waiting period for the refund of payments made into the social security fund. Those who withdrew their pension gave up further rights to retirement benefits and the possibility of returning to the Federal Republic of Germany.

4. A 1985 representative study (König *et al.* 1986) of all age groups of the foreign population finds 86.2 per cent working as manual labourers, about 20 per cent of these are skilled, and about 10.4 per cent of the foreign population are employed in white-collar occupations. According to this study, 22 per cent of the 15- to 24-year-old age group are employed as skilled workers, about 27 per cent of the men and 15 per cent of the women.

5. The observations in this section are based on several years of research with Turkish migrants in Berlin. The analysis rests on the findings of three main studies. The first is a 1975 study of 285 12- to 16-year-old Turkish, Yugoslav and German school children (Wilpert 1980). The second is a 1981 study of 430 Turkish and Yugoslav young people aged between 12 and 20 and 180 of their parents (Wilpert 1983). Both studies applied structured open interviews conducted in German and Turkish according to the preference of the respondent. The third study was launched within the framework of a project about the future prospects of migrant families. Ali S. Gitmez co-operated with the author in the collection of a series of narrative interviews of first- and second-generation Turks in Berlin, expert interviews and group discussions among second-generation youth and village chain migrants in Berlin. Riva Kastoryano has been associated with the follow-up of the narrative biographies of second-generation Turks in 1984.

6. The immigrant experience challenges traditional values and introduces complexity into childhood socialization patterns. This complexity is not simply a question of the conflict between the values of the old world and the new. Future time perspectives, long-term goal setting and the capacity to delay gratification are

behavioural strategies often considered missing among the lower classes. The vast majority of first-generation migrant workers have exercised these qualities during their migration experiences. Even when the educational style in the family remains authoritarian, which is likely since it may be considered both a characteristic of traditional families and the working conditions of the immigrant fathers, other childhood socialization experiences may counteract this. Migration introduces not only the aspiration for a better future, and initially at least the experience of relative success, it also disrupts the socialization process. As well as being a negative influence on family solidarity and the emotional security of children, it also upsets the normal mechanisms of social control. Two additional examples of changes in socialization patterns that are typical of 'guest' worker migration are: (a) the alienation from paternal authority that may occur through the fragmentation of the family; and (b) the new roles for children as mediators in the family, owing to better language skills than their parents in the new society. These conditions are likely to contribute to early experiences of self-direction.

Appendix

Table 5.A1   *Share of foreign pupils in Berlin schools in the 1979/80 and 1986/87 academic years*

School type	1979/1980		1986/1987	
	Total	Foreigners (per cent)	Total	Foreigners (per cent)
Elementary	114,688	16.3	90,260	24.0
Hauptschule (lower secondary)	19,152	27.9	10,032	39.4
Realschule (middle school)	22,729	5.5	15,179	16.9
Gymnasium (academic secondary)	50,312	3.6	41,076	8.3
Gesamtschule (comprehensive school)	29,681	6.4	24,186	20.8
Special schools	7,298	11.8	4,420	31.4
Sonderschule	3,056	6.0	2,667	15.5
Total	100%	12.4	100%	20.7
N	(246,916)	(30,613)	(188,343)	(138,298)

Source: *Senator für Schulwesen* (1986), 13.

Table 5.A2 *Socially insured active population in 1986, according to nationality, age groups and level of skills, per cent*

Age group years	1 Workers	2 White collar		Percentage of skilled workers in (1)
Germans				
15–19	63.7	36.3	= 100	9.6
20–24	53.4	46.5	= 100	46.9
25–29	47.6	52.4	= 100	53.7
30–34	43.0	57.0	= 100	53.2
35–39	43.0	57.0	= 100	52.3
40–44	42.9	57.1	= 100	50.0
45–49	50.3	50.0	= 100	46.6
50 and over	55.0	45.0	= 100	42.3
Total N = 19,138,560			= 100	
Foreigners				
15–19	88.3	11.6	= 100	4.4
20–24	87.6	12.3	= 100	19.6
25–29	82.0	18.0	= 100	23.8
30–34	80.0	20.0	= 100	24.0
35–39	81.6	19.4	= 100	29.6
40–44	84.0	16.0	= 100	29.9
45–49	87.0	13.0	= 100	28.2
50 and over	86.5	13.5	= 100	26.7
Total N = 1,591,547			= 100	

Source: calculations based on data from the *Bundesanstalt für Arbeit* (1986a), Table 60.23 (federal labour market).

References

Albrecht, C. and Schmid, G. (1985), *Beschäftigungsentwicklung und Qualifikationsstruktur in Berlin 1977–1983, Ein Vergleich mit 11 bundesdeutschen Ballungsregionen und 20 ausgewählten Arbeitsamtsbezirken*, Berlin: Wissenschaftszentrum, (discussion papers).

Autorengemeinschaft (1983), 'Der Arbeitsmarkt in der Bundesrepublik Deutschland 1983 und 1984 — insgesamt und regional', *Mitteilungen aus der Arbeitsmarkt-und Berufsforschung*, 325–44.

Beauftragte der Bundesregierung für die Integration der ausländischen Arbeitnehmer und ihrer Familienangehörigen (1986), *Bericht zur Ausländerbeschäftigung*, Bonn.

Bednarz, I. (1978), *Einstellung von Arbeiterjugendlichen zu Bildung und Ausbildung*, Münich: Deutsches Jugend Institut.

Bodenbender, W. (1977), 'Zwischenbilanz der Ausländerpolitik, türkische Kinder', in F. Ronneberger, *350,000 Türkenkinder in Deutschland*, Nürnberg: Nürnberger Forschungsvereinigung e.V.

Bundesanstalt für Arbeit (1973 and 1981), 'Socially insured employees in the Federal Republic of Germany in 1972 and 1980 according to age groups, sex and nationality' *Amtliche Nachrichten der Bundesanstalt für Arbeit (ANBA)*.

Bundesanstalt für Arbeit (1983), 'Share of foreigners according to sex in certain age groups of the total number of socially insured employees in the Federal Republic of Germany in 1982', *ANBA*, August.

Bundesanstalt für Arbeit (1984), 'Sozialversicherungspflichtig Beschäftigte nach Berufsgruppen und ausgewählten Berufsordnungen am 30 September 1983 im Bundesgebiet', *ANBA*, June, 898–9.

Bundesanstalt für Arbeit (1985), 'Die sozialversicherungspflichtig Beschäftigten von 1974 bis 1984', *ANBA*, May.

Bundesanstalt für Arbeit (1986a), *Beschäftigte Arbeitnehmer nach Alter und Stellung im Beruf, am 30.06.86*, Table 60.23.

Bundesanstalt für Arbeit, (1986b), *Sozialversicherungspflichtig Beschäftigte im Bundesgebiet am 30. September 1986*, Employment Statistics 11b4–4204.

Bundesanstalt für Arbeit (1986c) 'Sozialversicherungspflichtig Beschäftigte Frauen von 1977 bis 1985', in *Amtliche Nachrichten der Bundesanstalt für Arbeit*, September, 1303–17.

Bundesanstalt für Arbeit (1986d), 'Sozialversicherungspflichtig Beschäftigte Ende Marz 1986', in *Amtliche Nachrichten der Bundesanstalt für Arbeit*, November.

Bundesanstalt für Arbeit (1987a), 'Sozialversicherungspflichtig Beschäftigte Ende Juni 1986', in *Amtliche Nachrichten der Bundesanstalt für Arbeit*, March.

Bundesanstalt für Arbeit (1987b), 'Beschäftigte in beruflicher Ausbildung Ende Juni 1986', *Amtliche Nachrichten der Bundesanstalt für Arbeit*, April.

Bundesminister für Arbeit und Sozialordnung (Hrsg) (1986), *Integration der jungen Ausländer, Vorschläge des Koordinierungskreises Ausländische Arbeitnehmer*, Bonn, 1986.

Bundesminister für Bildung und Wissenschaft (1981), *Berufsbildungsbericht 1981*, Munich: Verlag Gersbach.

Bundesminister für Bildung und Wissenschaft (1986), *Berufsbildungsbericht 1986*, Bad Honnef: K.H. Bock Verlag.

Castles, S., Booth, H. and Wallace, T. (1984), *Here for Good, Western Europe's New Ethnic Minorities*, London: Pluto Press.

Deutsche Bundesbank, (1985) 'Überweisungen ausländischer Arbeitnehmer in ihre Heimatländer', in *Ausländer in Deutschland*, 4.

Dohse, K. (1981), *Ausländische Arbeiter und bürgerlicher Staat — Genese und Funktion von staatlichem Ausländerrecht vom Kaiserreich bis zur Bundesrepublik Deutschland*, Königstein: Verlag Anton Hain.

Dohse, K. (1983), 'Perspektiven der Arbeitsmarktentwicklung und der Ausländerpolitik', in Hamburger, F. (ed.), *Sozialarbeit und Ausländerpolitik*, Neuwied/Darmstadt: Hermann Luchterhand Verlag, 21–44.

Esser, H. (1986), *Kulturelle und ethnische Identität bei Arbeitsmigranten im Interkulturellen und intergenerationalen Vergleich*. Unpublished research report, Essen.

Fleischer, H. (1983), *Wirtschaft und Statistik*, 531–4.

Gitmez, A. and Wilpert, C. (1987), 'A Micro-Society or an Ethnic Community? Social Organization and Ethnicity amongst Turkish Migrants in Berlin', in: J. Rex, D. Joly. and C. Wilpert, *Immigrant Associations in Europe*, Aldershot: Gower.

Hecker, U. and Schmidt-Hackenberg, D. (1980), *Bildungs- und Beschäftigungssituation ausländischer Jugendlicher in der Bundesrepublik Deutschland*, Bundesinstitut für Berufsbildung, Berlin.

Hoffmann-Nowotny, H. J. (1973), *Soziologie des Fremdarbeiterproblems*, Stuttgart: Enke Verlag.

Jenschke, B. (1982), *Arbeit und Beruf: Chancen und Grenzen der Eingliederung von Ausländern in Berlin*, Vortrag anäßlich der gemeinsamen Tagung des Diozesanrates der Katholiken im Bistum Berlin (West) und der Evangelischen Kirche in Berlin-Brandenburg (Berlin West), on 26/27 February

König, P., Schultze, G., Wessel, R. (1986), *Situation der ausländischen Arbeitnehmer und ihrer Familienangehörigen in der Bundesrepublik Deutschland*, Repräsentativuntersuchung 1985, Bundesminister für Arbeit und Sozialordnung: Bonn.

Kühl, J. (1987), 'Zur Bedeutung der Ausländerbeschäftigung für die Bundesrepublik Deutschland', in: Reimann, Helga, Reimann, Horst (eds), *Gastarbeiter — Analyse und Perspektiven eines sozialen Problems*, Opladen: Westdeutscher Verlag

Kühn, H. (1979), *Stand und Weiterentwicklung der Integration der ausländischen Arbeitnehmer und ihrer Familien in der Bundesrepublik Deutschland*, Bonn: Beauftragte der Bundesregierung.

Kultusminister Konferenz (ed.) (1977), *Neufassung der Vereinbarung 'Unterricht für Kinder ausländischer Arbeitnehmer'. Beschlüse d. Kultusministerkonferenz vom 8.4.76*, Neuwied: Luchterhand.

Landesarbeitsamt Berlin (1986), 'Die Struktur der Arbeitslosigkeit in Berlin, (West), in den Altersgruppen unter 20 bzw 25 Jahren Ende September 1985', in *Statistische Mitteilungen*, 9 March

Lutz, B. (1982), 'Kapitalismus ohne Reservearmee? Zum Zusammenhang von Wirtschaftsentwicklung und Arbeitsmarktsegmentation in der europäischen Nachkriegszeit', in special issue of the *Kölner Zeitschrift für Soziologie und Sozialpsychologie*, **24**, 329–47

Mehrländer, U. (1978), *Einflußfaktoren auf das Bildungsverhalten ausländischer Jugendlicher*, Bonn.

Mehrländer, U. (1983), *Türkische Jugendliche – keine beruflichen Chancen in Deutschland?* Bonn: Verlag Neue Gesellschaft.

Mehrländer, U., Hofmann, R. et al (1981), *Situation der ausländischen Arbeitnehmer und ihrer Familienangehörigen in der Bundesrepublik Deutschland. Repräsentativuntersuchung '80*, Bonn: Der Bundesminister für Arbeit und Sozialordnung.

Mollwo, I. (1976), 'Berufliche Orientierung von Jugendlichen', *Mitteilungen aus der Arbeitsmarkt- und Berufsforschung*, **9** (4) 509–21

Münscher, A. (1979), *Ausländische Familien in der Bundesrepublik Deutschland - Familiennachzug und generatives Verhalten*. Materialien zum Dritten Familienbericht der Bundesregierung, Munich: Deutsches Jugend Institut.

Nikolinakos, M. (1973), *Politische Ökonomie der Gastarbeiterfrage. Migration und Kapitalismus*, Reinbek.

OECD (1981, 1984), *Sopemi*, Continuous Reporting System on Migration, Paris: OECD.

Piore, M. J. (1980), 'Dualism as a response to flux and uncertainty', in S. Berger and M. J. Piore, *Dualism and discontinuity in industrial societies*, Cambridge: Cambridge University Press, 23–54

Piore, M. J. (1979), *Birds of Passage: Migrant Labor and Industrial Societies*, Cambridge: Cambridge University Press.

Projektgruppe Jugendbüro (1977), *Subkultur und Familie als Orientierungsmuster*, Munich: Juventa Verlag.

Schober, K. (1981), 'Zur Ausbildungs- und Arbeitsmarktsituation ausländischer Jugendlicher in der Bundesrepublik Deutschland - gegenwärtige Lage und künftige Perspektiven', *Mitteilungen aus der Arbeitsmarkt- und Berufsforschung*, **1**, 11–21

Schober, K. (1983), 'Was kommt danach? Eine Untersuchung über den Verbleib der Teilnehmer an Maßnahmen zur Berufsvorbereitung und sozialen Eingliederung junger Ausländer (MBSE) des Lehrgangsjahres 1980/81 ein Jahr später', *Mitteilungen aus der Arbeitsmarkt- und Berufsforschung*, **2**, 137–52

Schober, K. (1985), 'Zur aktuellen Situation der Jugendlichen auf dem Arbeits- und Ausbildungsstellenmarkt', in *Mitteilungen aus der Arbeitsmarkt- und Berufsforschung*, **2**, 247–65.

Schober, K. (1986), 'Aktuelle Trends und Strukturen auf dem Teilarbeitsmarkt für Jugendliche', in *Mitteilungen aus der Arbeitsmarkt- und Berufsforschung*, **3**, 365–70.

Senator für Schulwesen, Jugend und Sport (1987), *Das Schuljahr 1986/87 in Zahlen*, Berlin.

Statistisches Bundesamt (1983), *Strukturdaten über Ausländer in der Bundesrepublik Deutschland*, Mainz: Verlag W. Kohlhammer.

Statistisches Bundesamt (1986), *Ausländer nach Altersgruppen, Familienstand und Aufenthaltsdauer*, Wiesbaden, Table 3.20.

Stegmann, H. (1981), 'Ausländische Jugendliche zwischen Arbeit und Beruf', *Mitteilungen aus der Arbeitsmarkt- und Berufsforschung*, 1–10.

Stegmann, H. and Kraft, H. (1983), 'Ausländische Jugendliche in Ausbildung und Beruf', *Mitteilungen aus der Arbeitsmarkt- und Berufsforschung*, **3**, 235–251.

Therborn, G. (1986), *Why some peoples are more employed than others: the strange paradox of growth and unemployment*, London: Verso.

Trommer, L. and Kohler, H. (1981), *Ausländer in der Bundesrepublik Deutschland*, Munich: Deutsches Jugend Institut.

Wagner, J. (1985), 'Arbeitsmarktegmentation und Beschäftigung im weltwirtschaftsin-duzierten Strukturwandel', in *Mitteilungen aus der Arbeitsmarkt- und Berufsforschung*, **3**.

Weische-Alexa, P. (1978), *Sozial-kulturelle Probleme junger Türkinnen in der Bundesrepublik Deutschland*, Cologne: Selbstverlag.

Wilpert, C. (1980), *Die Zukunft der Zweiten Generation. Erwartungen und Verhaltens-möglichkeiten ausländischer Kinder*, Königstein: Verlag Anton Hain.

Wilpert, C. (1982), 'Structural marginality and the role of cultural identity for migrant youth', in H. Korte (ed.), *Cultural identity and structural marginalization of migrant workers*, Strasbourg: European Science Foundation, 117–29.

Wilpert, C. (1983a), 'Minorities' influence on the majority: reactions of the majority in political, institutional and scientific spheres', in: C. Fried (ed.), *Minorities, Community and Identity*, Berlin: Springer, 177–90.

Wilpert, C. (1983b), 'Wanderung und Zukunftsorientierung von Migrantenfamilien', in: C. Wilpert and M. Morokvasig, *Bedingungen und Folgen internationaler Migration*, Berlin: Institut für Soziologie, Technische Universität Berlin, 3–274.

Wilpert, C. (1987), 'Zukunftsorientierungen von Migrantenfamilien: türkische Familien in Berlin', in: H. Reimann and H. Reimann, (eds) *Gastarbeiter*, Opladen: Westdeutscher Verlag.

6 Work and the Indeterminate Status of Young North Africans and Turks in Belgium: Integration into the Working Class or the Formation of a Sub Proletariat?

Albert Bastenier and Felice Dassetto

Introduction

What does it mean to be the daughter or son of a foreign worker? How does one become a member of the so-called second generation? In what way do the identity references of these young people become established and influence the process of their social and occupational integration?

These are some of the questions that will be considered in this chapter, where the cases of Turkish and north African young people in Belgium will be examined. The authors' interpretation of these cases profits from experience gathered in over ten years of research on the migratory phenomenon in Belgium, particularly with respect to the descendants of Italian migrants. This experience assists in evaluating the social dynamics of this phenomenon and allows a view of it from within the socio-historical framework of the waves of contemporary migration. In this way, it is hoped to compensate for the frequent sociological failures to integrate historical and generational processes and phases in the life-cycle in the analysis of social dynamics. The objective is also to provide a true sociological treatment of the factor 'youth' within the migratory process. The historical dimension is stressed as is the fact that these youth do not represent a homogeneous population. They can be differentiated according to 'migratory cycles', and these cycles involve sections of population that can be distinguished according to their origins and the historical moment they entered into the migratory process. These factors obviously have an impact on the emerging social trajectory of the actors.

The social historical context of the migration streams

Since this is a sociological analysis, its focus should not be limited to a conceptualization of the identity of youth of immigrant origin, as this reduces the issue to the subjectivity of the actors. The subjective construction of identity doubtlessly retains its significance, but it is of equal importance to investigate the structure of social relations that organize the individual trajectories of immigrants and the breadth of choices that are objectively accessible to them. This may ultimately include analyzing the way in which individual actors perceive these social relations and their own futures. One assumption that may be taken as a starting point is that these young descendants of immigrants are in the final phase of a process of social and geographical mobility, which by virtue of their fathers' entry into the labour force of an industrial society has introduced their families into the working class. Seen in this broader context, these young people represent, in fact, the first generation born into the working class. Thus, the present situation of the 'second generation' constitutes a sort of culmination of a process of transformation of the descendants of the immigrant labour force into becoming members of the proletariat.

In this case, the classical sociological concepts of stratification, mobility and equal opportunities seem altogether too narrow. In the case of young people of immigrant origins, it is necessary to investigate both geographical origins and destinations of the individuals as well as the particular economic and productive function of immigrant labour, such as their participation in the segmented labour market and the effects of their socio-cultural marginalization within the class structure. The concept of anthroponomical distribution, such as has been defined by Bertaux,[1] seems especially adequate since it takes into account the social logic that determines the mobilization and the allocation of individuals into their positions within the system of production and their societal relations in the widest sense of the term.

Migratory cycles and the transformation from immigrant labour to a settled proletariat

Immigration can be viewed as a process of becoming members of the proletariat. The migratory projects of individuals are formed when a work force is progressively uprooted from its traditional economic activity, often rural and agrarian, in order to become employed in various sectors of industrial societies, where there has been a need for a constant augmentation of the work force. What has been referred to as the 'primitive accumulation of proletarians' once satisfied by the rural European masses of the nineteenth and early twentieth centuries has now been replaced by international migrations.

After the end of the Second World War, there was not a sufficiently large working class available locally in Europe to provide the volume of labour that industrial production needed. The area of recruitment was therefore extended further into the Mediterranean basin, Africa and Asia. In the case of Belgium, the first wave of recruitment had in fact begun in the 1920s, and it started to intensify soon after the Second World War. Successive waves of immigrants entered the country from ever more distant geographical areas in fairly regular cycles. They were joined by their families, and generational reproduction occurred.

When analyzing the present-day Belgium migratory situation, it is important clearly to define the populations referred to within the historical context, which influences the conditions of their presence and their local integration. This is why the concept of 'migratory cycles' is used. This means the totality of the social and historical conditions that determine the process of their settlement. This process begins with the period of entry of the first wave of immigrants. Its completion is far less clear-cut. It takes the form of a gradual, progressive movement towards many and various forms of integration into the social structure of the receiving country. In contemporary Europe, this movement seems to coincide with the emergence of young adult descendants from migratory cycles on the social scene.

In Belgium, a first migratory cycle can be seen in the population of Italian origin, who were joined a little while later by those of Spanish origin. Today, the completion of a cycle that began with the social mobility of the 1960s is witnessed. Its integration with the 'state' was accomplished through a process of trans-nationalization, common in the member countries of the European Economic Community (EEC) during this period. The relationship of the nationals of these origins with the Belgian state was regulated within the EEC. At the same time, various fundamental features from their own cultures continued to thrive, encouraged by the many channels of communication available (transport and media). In this way, an affinity with the cultural references of their countries of origin could be maintained. This migratory cycle is characterized by a kind of social dissolution of immigrant way of life, along with permanent retention of their private cultural references. It could lead to a type of settlement just the opposite of that which Gordon (1964) was believed to have identified in the United States: leaving aside the nuances, Gordon speaks of acculturation without integration. Here, there is integration with only partial acculturation.

The second migratory cycle concerns primarily immigrants of Turkish and north African origin and takes place some time later, between 1960 and 1970. Its members are presently in the early stages of their settlement process. This migratory cycle is not supported by a context of social mobility as was the case in the previous period. On the threshold of the final phase of integration, it finds its way blocked by the current unemployment crisis. Moreover, the fact that these immigrants are from Muslim societies, and owing to the claims that Islam makes for the organization of society, the settlement process could resemble processes observed by Glazer and Moynihan (1975) in New York City. There they found the gradual transformation of ethnic associations into institutionalized interest groups permeating the surrounding social milieu. It should also be pointed out that a fairly high proportion of the Turkish immigrants of this second migratory cycle maintain the mentality of a temporary worker. They continue to have a strong sense of national identity and have a tendency to channel the maximum possible financial resources back to their country of origin, where they eventually hope to return. The insecurity and instability of this part of the population has quite unpredictable repercussions on the future of their migratory cycle – which is still in the process of completion.

Integration into the working class: objective and subjective affiliation
Historically, it is generally argued in Europe that the proletariat was initially formed when peasants turned towards industry as an alternative to their previous economic basis, which was in a state of collapse. The impulse that motivated these individuals – often whole families, sometimes even entire villages – was generally not hope, but necessity. The historian Kusznusci (1967) observes that what all these new workers share is that they do not consider factory work as something stable, but much more as 'occasional work which lasts'.

Like their predecessors, most of the immigrants initially considered their move to be a temporary one. Furthermore, they were encouraged in this idea by the 'migratory chain' policy laid down by the receiving countries within the framework of the Organization for Co-operation and Economic Development. (OECD) (1978).[2] This policy simply stated that the continued calls for new recruits to join the foreign labour force were cyclical. In this way, immigrants came to join an already established industrial proletariat, identifying themselves only partially with their subordinate working condition, and looking upon their geographical and occupational displacement as temporary.

The ideologically optimistic character of the temporary immigration policy explains, to a large extent, the connection made by many immigrants between geographical and social mobility. Quite

153

commonly, they perceived their migratory undertakings as purely instrumental – as part of a project to accumulate sufficient funds to allow them to return to the country of origin after a period of time, with the added bonus of improved social status. The influence of the myth of temporary immigration also helps the reader to understand one of the fundamental subjective aspects of the migratory phenomenon. Because they looked upon their condition purely as a temporary means to a material end rather than as a permanent, social existence, the immigrant families were able to justify sacrificing everything for the goal of returning to the country of origin. Whilst they were waiting, they consciously placed themselves in a state of indefinite 'limbo'.

Constant demands are placed on the running of any given social structure if it is to integrate different segments of the population. These demands were especially responded to in the settlement process of the first wave of European workers during the nineteenth century. However, despite the effects of a temporary immigration policy, European labour-importing societies believed for many years that their migratory politics could ignore these demands. So the question of the integration of these foreign workers was never discussed, as had happened in the case of the indigenous workers joining the proletariat. An attempt had been made to meet some of the demands made by the arrival of the first migratory cycle of Italian and Spanish immigrants, with ongoing integrative legislation within the EEC, but this was not repeated in the case of the second cycle (Morroccan and Turkish immigrants). It was not until the effects of the economic crisis in 1974 became clear that the debate on the need for their integration was begun. Nevertheless, it seems unrealistic to assume that the turnaround in the economic situation was the sole explanation for the change in migratory policy. It is also necessary to take into account the importance of problems related to the political administration of cultural and ethnic minorities, as well as to changes in public opinion, which became increasingly hostile towards the presence of foreigners. Perhaps the most important factor is that, when the importing countries decided to halt the migratory flow, the immigrants immediately began to settle where they were instead of returning to their countries of origin as expected. The authorities, once aware of the practically irreversible presence of immigrants, felt under pressure to undertake measures to influence the internal structure of the migrant population, to reduce their marginal position and foreign customs. Both in and out of the workplace, it was important that immigrants be integrated into the regular working class which, up until then, had not been seen as advantageous. So it is a mixture of socio-political, demographic and economic motives that explain the policy change in recent years and the necessity to integrate the immigrants into the working class.

In this same context, those labelled 'second generation' became the objects of an urgent, if rather belated, concern. This term, because of the disturbing educational, social, cultural and economic situation of the youth it describes, was immediately charged with strong emotions and subtly negative connotations. The term is also linked with a shift in the perceptions of minorities of foreign origin, at a time when local public opinion discovered that their presence was proving more and more likely to become a permanent feature. The stereotypes formerly associated with the presence of foreign workers were succeeded by new ones related to young descendants of immigrants, invading, omnipresent and terrifying in their numbers and their potential for social deviancy. The sudden emergence of this new dimension to the migratory phenomenon showed itself to be something more than an entry into a new phase in the history of European migrations and the ignorance nurtured for years of the effects of migration. Economic migration, even on a temporary labour basis limited to strictly economic ends, always leads to the migration of a people through the familial regroupings that this involves and the demographic dimension that follows.

In the following sections, the reader will see that the so-called 'second-generation problem' has become the unintended consequence of the process of integrating the immigrant population into the working class and its social reproduction.

The indeterminate status of offspring of immigrants — how comprehensive is their socialization into the working class?

First generation immigrants who joined the proletariat were, in most cases, uprooted peasants who remained such. The second generation, born or socialized at an early age in their parents' country of employment, should normally have been the first true members of the working class.

Despite their original temporary projects turning into permanent settlements, the immigrants of the first generation were basically an uprooted, transplanted people not engaged in pursuing a future in the country of temporary work. Abandoning their initial project to gain social recognition via reintegration into their country of origin, they often came to rely solely on the private sphere of their family relations. This group of workers did not primarily identify themselves with their occupational life as workers, perceiving it more instrumentally as a job than as a way of life. There can be no doubt that these 'temporary immigrants', who entered into 'provisional, temporary work which lasts', will continue to live like foreigners for whom the future exists elsewhere – even if this future takes place primarily on an imaginary level, with, for example, holidays in the country of origin acting as substitutes for the final return.

For their descendants, the second generation, the situation is, markedly different. Born or socialized in the context of industrial and urban society, they do not have a rural background, nor nostalgic bonds that join them with a society different from the one in which they live.

Therefore, for the vast majority of them, the subjective and objective future is to be found in the country of residence and their territorial anchoring is practically complete. However, the same cannot be said of their social integration into the working class and the system of production. These young people, influenced from their earliest youth by proletarian ways of life, should normally have completed the process of becoming working class begun by their parents. However, a series of specific factors distinguishing them from their native peers intervened, questioning this process.

The professional future of the son of a Belgian worker, in a relatively stable society with an established rhythm of social reproduction, is closely linked to the position of the father, to his material and social resources, and his capacity to profit from them or to squander them. The task of family and educational socialization is to guarantee this process, including the identification of occupational goals. As Lienard and Servais (1975) point out, the young from a working class milieu are encouraged to form realistic definitions of what is possible and impossible for them, of the permitted and the forbidden, the certitudes and incertitudes that they can expect in their social and professional future. This interpretation of an individual's own position and future, which is transmitted by daily socialization, is extremely effective, and can only be challenged by accidental counter-socialization. It is as though, over a long period of apprenticeship, the child of the working-class family comes to accept the position allotted to him in the social structure as his own, completely natural destiny.

It is less true for the daughter or son of an immigrant than for the offspring of an indigenous worker that to be born into proletarian conditions implies a naturally defined occupational destiny, a recognition of it and corresponding behaviour. It is no accident that observers of immigration and educators of all kinds are concerned about the identity of these young people, implying the belief that they escape socializing controls.

In fact, it is far from true that they escape socializing controls; rather it is their constant confrontation with a set of contradictions, reflecting the inconsistency of migratory policies, which translates into the indeterminate self-understanding of the immigrant community and its descendants.

With no clear vision of the future to inspire them to form a voluntary and collective plan, either to integrate or to return, the process of identity construction of these young people is based on complex plays of social understandings (Campioli 1977).[3] The young immigrant, unlike his indigenous peers, sees his entry into a world of work as a completely new beginning, as he identifies only partially with his occupational status, considering it 'provisory'. Further confusion stems from contradictory information on the foreign origins of his family, of their uncertain legal national status and the socio-cultural circumstances surrounding the initial migration.

It is because of these special circumstances, peculiar to the descendants of immigrants in the various dimensions of their social positioning, that their future may be more 'open' than is the case for youth of the indigenous working class, despite certain less favourable conditions. To be 'open' should be understood here not in the sense of an infinity of possibilities, but as the manifestation of a 'discontinuity' in the relationship between the parents and their children.[4]

As far as the domain of educational socialization is concerned, it can be seen as the means by which society imposes a set of objective norms on its youth. Here young foreigners are not only supposed to be prepared for the accomplishment of their future occupational tasks, but are also forced to distance themselves from the culture and framework of family relations. From numerous studies carried out on the academic performance of immigrant children, it is known that their school life does not generally help to liberate them from the completely inferior position that their parents fill on the occupational ladder, as is the case in children from the lowest scale of the indigenous working class.

Therefore, the great majority of young descendants of immigrants are seen as belonging to the working class, with no real occupational qualifications. However, it is not only from this point of view that the school makes a special mark on these youth. The norms governing the socio-cultural universe communicated by the family are also undermined. Because of the largely multi-ethnic educational atmosphere in areas with a high proportion of immigrants, this undermining is not generally counterbalanced by the real possibility of a new cultural identity. Even if the school succeeds in attaining a reasonable level of socialization of young immigrants, relating their aspirations to a certain degree with those of indigenous youth of comparable social status, it also contributes to identity fragmentation which is related to the discontinuity and indetermination, as mentioned above.

Once the period of primary and secondary socialization are completed, a crucial moment for the social integration of these young foreigners arises with their transition into the world of work. Unfortunately, this decisive entry takes place at the very time when economic crisis exposes them, more than anyone else, to the risks of unemployment.

Because of the discontinuity in their itinerary and their particular historical situation within migratory cycles, these youth became what might be termed an 'irregular proletariat'. Their geographical settlement is not accompanied by a clear social integration and the purely linear pursuit of a certain route is no longer evident.

Social roles, occupational orientations and identity choices of young north Africans and Turks in Belgium

The purpose of the study carried out among young north Africans and Turks in Belgium was to obtain a more accurate picture of their special situation and their self-image in their transition from adolescence to adulthood upon entering the job market and/or when they made plans to marry.

The sample

As already mentioned, this study follows on from other studies conducted about the second generation, which concentrated in particular on the Italians (Dassetto and Bastenier 1982). Therefore a far greater background knowledge was brought to the analysis of the following interviews than if their cases had simply been taken in isolation. The present study is based on a sample of 33 young subjects (from 19 to 33 years of age) originating from north African (20) and Turkish (13) families. All belonging to the second generation, they were either born in Belgium or arrived there before the age of 10. Their formal education completed, they were either at work (22, of whom 4 undeclared) or unemployed (11). This study includes 17 young men and 16 young women, 15 of whom are single and 18 married. This sample should be reasonably reliable, even if not fully representative. The observations were gathered through a series of in-depth, semi-directive interviews. During these discussions, the subjects expressed themselves freely on topics which were suggested to them. Topics chosen were those likely to supply useful information on the subjects' social trajectory, the conscious or unconscious strategies they adopt to cope with their present situation and the self-image during this period of their life, that is their identity orientations at a time when, leaving adolescence, they become settled into the role of an adult social actor.

The backgrounds and migratory goals of the families

All families interviewed had emigrated between the years 1962 and 1973: towards the start of this period in the case of the Morroccans (from 1962 to 1969), and a little later in the case of the Turks (from 1964 to 1973). It is therefore clear that they belong to the most recent migratory cycle in Belgium.

The occupational origins of the fathers point clearly towards their reasons for emigration. Agricultural workers, small businessmen or craftsmen, virtually all of them looked upon this move as a means of overcoming the economic difficulties they were faced with in the country of origin. Their move to Belgium meant an entry into the lowest rung of the waged work force in the mining, industry and construction sectors. Almost every one of them saw this migration as part of a plan, to earn enough money to allow them to return to their country of origin, entering hopefully in the tertiary sector, and thereby becoming upwardly mobile. Their 'provisory' proletarian existence in Belgium generally lasted longer than imagined and a series of new constraints (among them the education of their children) led to them setting aside their aspirations for return. The economic crisis beginning in 1973 only served to encourage settlement in Belgium, due to the reduced likelihood of a successful return and the risk of losing the relative advantages they now had in the receiving country. The prospect or the reality of unemployment has certainly made the situation even more insecure for the most recent arrivals. This prospect has perhaps encouraged others immediately to carry out occupational plans that they had not intended to put into operation until returning to their country of origin – their dream, for example, of becoming a small businessman or restaurant-owner.

The families of each interviewee are in the process of transforming their original migratory projects, and they have entered the early stages of settlement in Belgium.

The descendants of immigrants — during the formative years

The educational position of the interviewees confirms what numerous investigations in Belgium and elsewhere in Europe (Bastenier, Dassetto and Fonck 1986) have already revealed about the schooling and vocational training of foreign youths: that their general educational integration, even at the primary level, is extremely problematic. Failures are numerous, and many of these youths do not even obtain a diploma certifying completion of the

159

elementary cycle. This initial gap has serious repercussions when they reach the level of vocational training, where they continue to encounter difficulties similar to those they experienced in elementary school. It also appears to be their failure and boredom at elementary school level which leads these young people to inferior branches of vocational training. Moreover, a large number of them do not complete this training, opting to drop out without diplomas.

Beyond this confirmation of the failures of the educational system with regard to foreign youths, the study reveals the feelings of these young people towards schooling. These include their opinion of the years they spent in education and of the family conditions which supported or discouraged the acquisition of occupational qualifications. These are a series of elements in the socialization of these youths which seem to have a considerable influence on their cultural choices and future identities. One surprising aspect that north African and Turkish young adults remember about their educational years is the importance their parents seemed to attach to their schooling. A considerable effort is invested by immigrant families in the instruction of their children, even beyond the level of compulsory education. The demands of the children's education are often quoted as the reason for postponing their return to the country of origin. This is even more true for girls than for boys, as the female children usually continue their studies for longer and have greater educational ambitions than the males. Is this an attempt on the part of the young women to become more highly qualified in order to gain greater autonomy from their family, who will try to retain control over their female offspring? Or is it an attempt on the part of the parents to put off the daughters' entry into the work place for as long as possible? Both assumptions may be true.

Very few of the young people claim to have enjoyed a truly supportive atmosphere during their educational years. Sometimes the educational aspirations of the parents for their children help the family to move towards success and to realize its ambitious objectives. More often, however, there is a considerable dissonance between the parents' approving attitude towards school and what the real context of family life actually permits the youngsters to accomplish. Looking back and analyzing this period, the interviewees generally summed up in the following contradiction: the parents regularly stressed the importance of a good education but the circumstances of the family life offered no real support. Many went on to state that the school and the teachers did nothing but aggravate the situation. This reinforced still more their wish to avoid school, first through absenteeism and subsequently by starting work. Almost all of them in retrospect regret having wasted this time.

A few who would have liked to pursue some kind of training gave in to the parents' wishes for them, in the case of young women to marry and in the case of young men to go out and earn a supplementary income for the family. They unanimously felt that they did not benefit from the structure and guidance they needed during these years of their lives. This opinion was summed up rather well in the expression used by a young Turk: 'I was like a sheep without a shepherd!'

What also becomes apparent from the interviews is the extent to which the uprooting experience of emigration weakened or fractured the immigrant family unit. It disturbed the model of the traditional, rural family, leaving it without a coherent strategy towards education. Its social and economic condition usually prevent it from being able to support viable education plans for its children. In other words, the mechanisms of traditional socialization through the family can no longer function efficiently. Furthermore they have not been replaced by others – by the school for example, which might have served as a substitute for this deficit. Most of the young north Africans and Turks have had a very dissatisfying educational experience, ending rapidly with a premature attempt to enter the work force. Sometimes, the economic demands of the family still the educational plans that they initially had. Family ties remain important to these youngsters, their working life continuing to be modelled on the classical idea of duty to the family.

Finally, the interviews seem to indicate that these young people very rarely had the opportunity during their education to aim towards a specific type of employment. Of course, there were several cases where very ambitious aspirations for the future were declared (to become a doctor, a managing director, and so on), but these ambitions were not coupled with a concrete sense of reality and true motivation towards their fulfilment. Apart from these few cases, where the difference between expectations and real practical possibilities were not taken into account, attitudes towards training are generally determined in terms of the material gains that work, of whatever kind, brings with it, rather than in terms of a desire for true occupational integration.

Before this account of the influences active during the socialization period of young foreigners is concluded, a discovery from another study should be mentioned (Dassetto and Bastenier 1984). The system of organization of local education and the legal status given to the major religious confessions in Belgium permits that nearly 50 per cent of young north Africans and Turkish pupils receive religious instruction in the Islamic faith within the regular educational establishments. It is not possible to give a precise interpretation of the impact this has on young people of Muslim origin. However, this reality must not be overlooked when considering the process of their identity development. Other research conducted on Islamic institutions and organizations in Belgium indicates that there exist a number of attempts to develop programmes to re-activate Muslim and Arabic culture. This, combined with the system of educational organization in Belgium, creates quite an ambiguous situation, since it adds to the diffusion of at times quite contradictory cultural messages for these youths.[5]

Situation and attitudes towards waged labour
Observations of the initial aspirations the young north Africans and Turks express upon their entry into the labour market and the comments they make later about their experiences with waged work has led to the conclusion that they are almost unanimous about the value they place on work 'in itself', but that they are much less ready to attach importance to the actual daily experience of working life. In this way, they are not much different from their indigenous peers. An hypothesis advanced by Ruquoy and Hiernaux (1986) about young Belgians could be equally true for young foreigners: the problem is not primarily that young people devalue waged work, but rather that the actual work offered disappoints the positive image they had held of work as such.

In fact, is it possible to speak about the world of work today when youth employment has become so irregular? When it has become common for young immigrants as well as their indigenous counterparts to experience periods of work followed by periods of unemployment?[6] Given the precarious condition of young workers, work itself is no longer experienced as a stabilizing entry into adult life.

The authors' main argument is that, in the case of young immigrants, waged work offers less opportunity for becoming members of the proletariat than in the case of their native peers. Firstly, some typical attitudes expressed on this matter by young immigrant workers will be examined.

A first type of attitude, which seems to be as frequent among young men as young women, reflects the early wish and even the urgency with which they began to work. For them, this step represented either a means of breaking with the world of school, the place of their first social disappointment, or a means rapidly to gain money to satisfy a certain level of consumption. Work was also, however, frequently viewed as a means of gaining autonomy *vis-à-vis* the family. This was especially true for young women. These forms of motivation are, of course, not mutually exclusive. The deepest disappointments were experienced among youth of this first-attitude type during the cyclical crisis, when the number of jobs was greatly reduced. Young men, especially, experienced difficulty in finding a job, in the first place. Then the unstable periods, work followed by periods of unemployment, came as a bitter blow, becoming the source of feelings of helplessness and the perception of social rejection. These feelings are more subtle in the case of young immigrant women, because, despite labour market difficulties, their determination to maintain their autonomy *vis-à-vis* the family is normally stronger than their feelings of disappointment.

A second type of attitude, more common among the young men, gives the impression that they feel that their entry into the labour market was forced upon them. This meant either that they felt the social situation of the family offered them no other alternative, or that they experienced pressure from their parents, especially their fathers, who found their children more and more difficult to control and believed that work would have a stabilizing influence on them: work stopped them from hanging around on the street. A third reason given was that their work would contribute a new financial source for the family ventures, buying a flat or some other joint investment. The experiences gained during the first year of work did not leave a different impression from that observed in the preceding attitude type: work with a dubious level of security, at times undeclared, interrupted by periods of unemployment resulted in bitter feelings. In other words, this explains their weak social integration into the world of work.

The third and last type of attitude seems to be the least common one. Entry into work was experienced as the normal culmination of a period of education. Here, subsequent experiences in the work place are more positive, as these youth seem to be satisfied with the beginning of their occupational life, and they believe that it will serve as a basis for their personal mobility in the future.

For the first two attitude types, the years immediately following the youths' entry into the labour market were filled with disappointment. Their experience of the world of work (working conditions, social relations, remuneration) and the resulting self-esteem produced only disenchantment, disillusionment and, in one case, disgust. Most of these young foreigners end up with a rather cynical viewpoint of work: it has no other value than the money it provides – a means to a living.

The aspirations of young men: work or wages?
From the above accounts of experiences in the working world, it

would be too difficult to draw any definite conclusions on what is special or relevant about the attitude of young north Africans or Turks towards work and occupations. What is striking, however, within the group of interviewees is the relatively high number of them whose profound dissatisfaction with their condition as waged workers leads them to form plans – realistic or not – to escape from their subordinate, waged conditions. For some, this plan entails becoming self-employed as a shopkeeper, restaurant or garage owner, hairdresser, heating engineer, and so on. For others, it is a matter of 'joking around',[7] trying to escape the constraints of the working environment, which they consider meaningless. In this case, the activities involved range from repeated absenteeism to 'taking things into their own hands', which, because of the lack of satisfying occupational opportunities, leads to underground economic activities.

The extent of rejection or alienation from work varies in intensity according to the cases and the particular social groups involved. It is understandable that in a group so lacking in occupational qualifications and, therefore, so exposed to the risks of unemployment, the persuasive power of the arguments of the agents of socialization about the value of work become less and less effective. Nevertheless, even in the numerous cases where the young interviewees were resigned to the experience of work as a kind of 'occupational nomadism', interrupted by periods of inactivity, every one of them rejected the alternative of 'non-work' which unemployment represents.[8] This is even true for those who 'taking things into their own hands' or who by 'joking around' manage for better or worse to survive a period of social latency which delays their settling into adulthood. Thus, on the whole, work is still valued in the eyes of the young north Africans and Turks, despite their negative experiences. If this is so, where does the discontinuity in the lives of young foreigners occur, and how far are they from their integration into the working class?

It is important to emphasize that, for a certain number of young north Africans and Turks, in the process of completing the last phase of the migratory cycle in Belgium, the situation really is very different from that of their predecessors. Occupational integration was assured for the latter, and they could retain their cultural identity with at least a prospect, if only a symbolic one, of returning to the country of origin should their migratory goals fail. This is no longer true for a very high proportion of the young generation, who enter adulthood during a period of severe unemployment. Now, those who, in principle, should have moved into the labour force are really faced with the very likely prospect of unemployment. A new kind of marginality is added to their political estrangement and the fragmentation of their cultural references. How is it possible to speak of social integration of these young people when an essential element, their integration into the economy, is missing? The marginalization process of a large number of young north Africans and Turks with more than half of them unemployed becomes more a question of the potential formation of a sub-proletariat than integration into the working class.

It seems that, when some essential elements of identity construction, such as civic loyalty and emotional attachment, are considered, the potential formation of a sub-proletariat is a factor that should not be disregarded in this analysis. These youths may tend to be drawn into a 'drifting stratum' of a surplus population without stable ties to the working world. This is sociologically significant, less because of the increased instability of their condition or their poverty than because of the new element of indetermination this situation introduces into the already complex process of their identity construction. As already mentioned, the lack of employment prospects has led some interviewees to opt for 'taking things into their own hands' as solutions to their dead-end situations. According to them, this simply means drifting into underground activities. However, the possibility cannot be ruled out that, in a certain number of cases, this social drift may lead to a more marked social deviance. This may simply be the pursuit of immediate gratification to gain at least the symbols of success through some form of deviant behaviour. In extreme cases of social marginality, such behaviour may be a final attempt at social communication, the only apparent alternative perceived open to these youth.

The tendency towards forming a sub-proletariat relates, however, to only a fraction of the young population mentioned here. It appears that it is just as important to consider the situation of those who turn to self-employment as a means of escape from a job that they find thoroughly dissatisfying. This particular way of seeking a way out from an occupational condition in which young foreigners feel basically 'present but absent' distinguishes them clearly from their indigenous peers. Of course, many young Belgians also experience negatively the working conditions they face. Although strictly comparative data is not available, they do seem, on the whole, to be less dissatisfied with their condition than the young foreigners interviewed. More importantly, the reaction of indigenous young Belgians to this situation is appreciably different to that of the interviewees, in that their first goal is not to leave their waged condition in favour of a non-traditional type of work, but rather to progress to a different waged employment which is satisfying, stable and secure.[9] In other words, the economic crisis has contributed to the instability of the working life of all youth, but more so for the descendants of immigrants than for natives. This explains why their integration into the working class is blocked.

It is necessary to go beyond this first observation and take a close look at the different ways young foreigners react to the present obstacles in the labour market, which all youth face to a greater or lesser degree. The young foreigners display a greater capacity than their indigenous peers to foresee potential alternative occupational futures for themselves. Of course, the social realism of the strategies that they develop could be questioned, as could whether they will achieve an occupational position other than that which would seem to be their legacy, taking into consideration the social trajectory begun by their parents. Since no one has any idea what form their occupational activity will ultimately take, the possibility cannot be excluded that at present nothing more than the sort of moratorium is being witnessed. This may, according to some authors,[10] affect the transition from one phase in the life-cycle to the next for almost all youths, thereby prolonging the period of insecurity before reaching a more or less definitive occupational integration. It is also necessary to examine the influence the family environment has on the occupational plans and the identification of young foreigners with work. Their perceptions of work are not initially and completely based on the experience of work itself but can be largely attributed to the values and norms instilled by primary socialization, that is by the family. If the dissatisfaction with waged work leads young foreigners much more than young Belgians to refuse to see themselves as belonging to the working class condition of waged labour, it is felt that this must be seen in relation to the cultural orientations of the family. The family does little to encourage them in the direction of a condition with which they themselves identify only partially.

Is it the instrumental nature of the parents' distance to waged work that weakens their children's image of work as a disciplined and valued activity? Does it, thereby, also weaken the desirability of integration into the working class?

How and why first-generation immigrants consider the type of jobs they entered as being temporary employment rather than a permanent condition has already been discussed. Their aspiration to regain social status by returning to their country of origin was aimed precisely at moving into non-working class occupations. Could it be that the second generation has adopted the original plans of their parents, who themselves failed to complete their objectives and to achieve the level of mobility hoped for? Whatever the case may be, many young immigrants strive to avoid joining the working class, and contrary to what some might have expected, this is with the encouragement of their families.

Working women and family roles
One aspect of this study in particular concerns the potential for significant changes in the roles and status of immigrant women when they enter the world of work. This adds another dimension to the identity choices associated with work, and teaches something about socio-cultural practices, as well as something about the choices and strategies that lead to the occupational behaviour of women. Also, reading between the lines of what these young women say about the influence that work may have had on their family roles and status, a glimpse is caught of male reactions to this situation.

Almost all of the north African and Turkish young women interviewed had been living in Belgium for most of the period of their primary socialization. The plans and problems of these young women were, as well, very similar to their indigenous peers. These are not, however, very uniform and in their narrative interviews they vacillate between two extremes of what is often referred to as 'traditional' and 'modern'.

The complexity of their situation and the contradictions in some of their aspirations reveal a dramatic change with respect to the statuses and roles of their mothers. This observation in no way justifies, however, the facile assumptions that the culturalist approach has often made about immigrant women. Basically, the culturalist approach makes generalizations founded on the traditional image of women held in European societies, thus they assume that the main preoccupation of women of foreign origin would be to become a little more 'modern'. Whereas, it will become apparent, things are a bit more complex.

The fact that immigration may bring about a change for some of these young women compared to the status of their mothers should not negate the role that material necessity plays in the transformation of traditions. This is one source of explanation for the hesitancy and the contradictions that these young women may express. The critical way in which they view their parents' trajectory and their positive or negative feelings towards the cultural background of their family, which they never completely reject, demonstrates both the distance that exists betweem them and their culture of origin as well as their resistance, or even refusal, to accept the standard feminine models common in Belgian society.

Initially, most young north African and Turkish women, when considering the image of the woman they hope to become, compare their lives with what they know or imagine about the lives of their mothers. The vast majority stress their desire to avoid a life like the one their mothers had. In a discussion of the question of 'emancipation', young foreign women share some of the concerns with their indigenous peers: the desire not to be tied down by housekeeping and childrearing, and the wish not to be dependent on their husbands.

At the same time, the discussion of these issues is coloured by their tendency to dramatize the position of their mothers, who are described as 'slaves', culturally 'imprisoned', and 'submitting' to this because immigration was a male project, and they did nothing more than to follow as dependents. One or two openly declare, whilst others only hint at, the fact that they reject their mothers' life style partly because immigration was an experience of submission which left them impoverished. In the country of origin, the women are freer and may be more 'modern thinking' than those living here, as migration often brought about a kind of cultural 'standstill'. During the initial period of migration, the women of the first generation did nothing but hang their destiny on their husbands' plans. They had no personal projects that might have helped them to cope with the total transformation of their living conditions and the sudden loss of their old frames of reference and traditional networks of social relations. Much less 'active' than in the country of origin and often confined to the home – most of them possessing minimal cultural knowledge – they were destined to become guardians of the old family values and traditions which had been cut off at their source. The only ones who managed to find a way out of this initial situation were those who went out to work themselves. However, the decision to take this step was almost always made because of the material needs of the family or following a broken marriage.

Rather than viewing the way these young women see themselves as a simple move from 'tradition' towards 'modern thinking', equal importance should be given here to the effects of the socio-cultural constraints operant in the migratory milieu, from which the young women are trying to free themselves.

If this is taken into consideration, it is easier to understand what motivates young foreign women to reach quickly the status of working women. Rather than run the risk of being forced into early marriage and a situation similar to that of their elders, they seek to integrate themselves into the surrounding society, which the preceding generation of immigrant women failed to do. However, such integration into industrialized and tertiary urban societies can no longer be achieved by simply assuming a role within the context of extended family solidarity. It demands that the individual has her own source of economic security, providing not only independence from the family but also the freedom to move around within a consumer economy. In order to adopt the behaviour appropriate to this type of society, it is vital to have the appropriate means at a person's disposal.

This is obviously not an exhaustive account of the female interviewees' reasons for entering waged work. The simple necessity of providing for the elementary needs of family life was certainly also a reason for them going out to work. It is striking how little importance they attached to this aspect of the situation, few of them mentioning it spontaneously. It is also significant that, unlike the young men, they did not express their feelings about their actual experiences of work. Instead these young women gave priority to the advantages they saw in the fact of working, which can be summarized as: coming into contact with others; getting out of a closed environment; breaking away from family supervision; emancipating themselves; taking an active part in society; having their own money; being considered as an equal; and doing what they want. From this set of statements it can be seen that work is the strategic instrument of personal independence for these women, as well as being a means of social integration. Apart from the social implications of entering work, what was discovered about the beginnings of a medium- or long-term plan for settling into the condition of waged work? Since the number of interviewees was limited, the response to this question must be cautious. Nevertheless, the answer seems to be 'no'. Almost all the young women interviewed are employed in subordinate positions with no real prospects for advancement. Furthermore, there is little relation between the positions they occupy and their basic occupational training (if they had one). Most of them express deep regret at not having completed schooling, which would have made further training for a different, more qualified type of employment possible. They 'work', but have no specific occupational plans. Most of them aspire to nothing more than occupational stability in the lower echelons of the hierarchy. The desire these young female foreigners may once have had to obtain social mobility by means of a 'real' occupation is not seen as realistic for themselves, and a number of them blame this on the young children they have or plan to have. When this topic was raised during the interviews, many of them confessed their fundamental belief that the role of the woman is really to take care of her children.

In this way, as though torn between their desire for personal autonomy and social integration on the one hand, and returning to what they consider to be the 'true' female role on the other, these young women seem to confirm what the statistics indicate.[11] Almost one-half of women who are economically active started work at an early age, but did not carry on beyond the age of 25 years. Thus, they did not become settled into a waged condition. They left work after about ten years to return to the family and children.

The occupational activity of young north African and Turkish women usually has only a fleeting importance, being part of a temporary plan. However, it does strengthen their economic role at a decisive time in their lives, providing them with the personal independence necessary to negotiate their role and status within the family. These negotiations with their partners often prove harsh and only partially successful, frequently resulting in a number of them having to take on the traditional role once more, at the same time as continuing their occupational activities. The fact remains, however, that the respective roles of the family members have been questioned, stimulating a phase of redefinition. Nevertheless, it is still striking how many young immigrant women who work seem careful not to disturb the old equilibrium of the male and female roles within the family. This reticent attitude on their part partially reflects the profound attachment these young women have towards traditional family values. This reticence also goes hand in hand with their difficulties in finding ways of coping with the new equality in power relations within the couple itself. So the attachment that practically all young north African and Turkish women express for family values – even if they see room for improvement in their relative roles and statuses – leads to the conclusion that their passage through a period of waged labour was never envisaged with the prospect of permanence. It was more a question of a temporary financial support with a view towards better negotiating their entry into the reality of the family, which, in the process of migration, changes from its traditional form to the nuclear type centred on the dynamics of the couple.

Conclusion

At the beginning of this chapter, the question was posed as to how the identity references of young foreigners form and influence their occupational integration. The empirical data emerging from this study of young north Africans and Turks, and the theoretical nature of the framework within which it has been placed, obviously do not allow an exhaustive and definitive answer to this initial question. Also, given the present state of the sociology of migration, the problem of identity remains far too vague and undefined for the authors to claim to have a view that ignores analytical information on the social structure and on history. Young descendants of immigrants pursue their destiny not only in the historical continuity of their ethnic group of origin, but also in that of the society in which the process of geographical and social mobility, beginning with their parents' migration, reaches completion. This process takes place within migratory cycles whose particular forms have an influence on the social trajectory of the actors.

The young north Africans and Turks on whom the study is based are descendants of the latest migratory cycle towards Belgium. The socio-cultural traits belonging to their original nationality groups, as well as historical circumstances at the time when they are in transition on to work and adulthood, have a significant impact on their identification process. As far as the young men are concerned, there can be no doubt that the objective situation of the labour market hits them very hard. Through lack of work, almost all of them are confronted with the contemporary insecurity of the condition of young workers and consequently with the absence of the socializing and stabilizing influence work should bring.

Despite everything, the more or less satisfactory occupational integration of a certain number of the foreigners will be achieved. Even if this process has to take longer than expected, they will end up joining the working class, since there are few other alternatives. However for another not inconsiderable number of these youths, what should have been a decisive step in the construction of their identity will in fact only lead to their entry into a chaotic process of sub-proletarianization, the long-term result of which is not known. The remaining fragments of ethnic, cultural and social references still accessible to these youth can combine in many different forms, resulting in unexpected patterns of behaviour. These might at times lie outside the realm of the normal; at other times be simply aimed towards the acquisition of the symbols of social recognition, which every human existence requires.

The readers' attention was particularly drawn to a further section of the young north African and Turkish population, for whom the insecurity of the employment market and/or their dissatisfaction with contemporary conditions of waged work has reactivated certain elements of familial socialization. It was precisely this socialization that never encouraged them to establish themselves as workers. The members of this particular group, more frequently than their indigenous peers, seek self-employment. This ties in with the original migration goals of their parents – to use geographical mobility to achieve social mobility.

As for the young women, what distinguishes them from the men is the way in which they make use of their occupational activity to improve their position when the time comes for their future marriages to be discussed. North African and Turkish families still keep a close control over the matrimonial destiny of their female children. However, in their identity formation and occupational pursuits while negotiating for a change from 'tradition' to 'modern thinking', they make quite sure that their work does not too much disturb the balance between masculine and feminine roles within the family. There are two possible explanations for this: firstly, the strong influence still exerted by the image of the mother; or, secondly, the difficulty these young women experience in adapting to the new roles their work brings about within the nuclear-type family, which their socialization has not prepared them to assume.

The final question concerns determining whether the peculiarities that distinguish the process of identity construction among foreign youth when they enter the world of work are simply a consequence of the present economic crisis, or whether something else – more serious and more permanent – lies behind this. In the case of the young adult descendants of Turkish and north African immigrants, it is clear that the external factor of the current economic crisis intervenes in a powerful way. The situation of 'no-work' that they face quite simply deprives a number of them of a normal form of social interaction, which is a vital element in defining a person's social position. They are thus led into forming a kind of sub-proletariat. Appeals that youths in these circumstances sometimes make to social and cultural resources might be considered as more of a form of reactive behaviour, and thus more accidental than substantial. Interpretations are more difficult with respect to those young people who, rather than drifting into an undefined sub-proletarian status, seek a social position other than that of a waged labourer. In this case, the identity to which they aspire seems to be much more powerful than that which they have inherited. The persistence with which a large number of these people express a desire for a future outside of the working class condition ought to prompt questions about ways in which certain immigrant ethnic minorities might belong to the local society during their process of settlement.

Notes

1. The exact meaning of the French word *anthroponomique* cannot be translated directly into English. Therefore, Bertaux's (1977) definition is quoted here:

   > The social logic which sets social actors into motion, and which leads them to settle into the positions (of work and status) which they are to occupy in relation to the universe of production and the social relationships associated with this universe.

2. The OECD's doctrine of the 'migratory chain' is literally taken from the 1978 OECD document entitled *La chaîne migratoire*.

The notion of the migratory chain has been progressively elaborated upon by the OECD as an analytical model and an operational instrument, and has become the central element of its main doctrine on matters of international migration. This notion indicates the various sequences in the migratory process (departure, immigration, settlement in the receiving country, possibly return to the country of origin etc...); the relationship between these various sequences; and the cumulative effect the complete process has on the social and economic plan. (OECD 1978, p. 5).

As early as 1975, the OECD was using the term 'the organization of the migratory chain' to describe the 'chain of effects' of migration (OECD 1975).

3. Campioli, who has studied the educational career of the children of immigrants, finds that:

Rather than growing up with the comfort and calm acceptance which leads to a reproduction of occupational choices, the children of immigrant workers witness the traumatizing experience of transplantation (rupture, early experience of traumatizing events). Sharing the resources and the difficulties of their families, they sense the confusion of parents faced with situations where knowledge acquired in another culture is worthless (their fathers communicate a fundamental anxiety), ineffective, amusing to others (lack of credibility, prestige). Very early on they are forced to take initiative; to help their parents in a series of steps, assume the responsibilities which more rapid learning of the language and other factors of a new milieu impose upon them (early maturity). On the other hand, the parents insist less on an attempt to adapt to an established world than on the need to succeed within a society in evolution. They point towards their own pasts as proof of the efforts they themselves made in this direction (acceptance of the need to innovate, cohesion of the family). This means that resources must be effectively used for education. Moreso than in other situations, the children make an important share of the decisions which concern them because of the ignorance of their parents. It is important to determine the factors or persons of reference which influence them (an individual or a group they use as model, whose norms they adopt and who provide a basis for judgement of themselves and others). These can channel or deviate the influence of the family situation. The initial success in school which takes on more importance here is experienced not as something banal, but as an achievement, increasing the desire for success, reinforcing self-esteem, raising the level of aspirations and encouraging ambitious objectives. (Campioli 1977).

4. To some extent, this echoes the problematic of Bourdieu (1974) when he says:

The attitude towards the objective future of the heritage (understood here in the economic, social or cultural sense) is itself a function of the investment strategies of previous generations — that is to say, the present and potential position of the agent or group of agents affecting the distribution of capital (economic, cultural and social), understood as having power over the instruments of production and reproduction. (ibid.)

5. Teachers of the Islamic religion are selected by representatives of the country of origin, with no real control by the Belgian government. This often leads to the appointment, for ideological and economic reasons, of propagandists with a strong or reactionary identity with the country of origin.

6. In Belgium, the growth in unemployment has greatly accelerated amongst the under-25 age group in recent years: in 1974 this group represented 20.5 per cent of the total unemployed; in 1984, they exceeded 30 per cent. Foreign origin is a supplementary variable that affects the volume of unemployed among

the young: whereas an index of 100 in 1974 moved to 546 in 1984 for the whole of the under-25 age group, the same indices moved from 100 to 703 in the case of foreign youth. At the end of 1984, 29 per cent of job seekers were under 25 years old; 42.4 per cent were of foreign origin. This increased to 50 per cent in the case of young Morroccans and to 56 per cent in the case of Turks (Bastenier, Dassetto and Fonck 1986).

7. The French expression *ruser avec la vie*, here translated as 'joking around', is an expression used by young immigrants to indicate that they are attempting to obtain the financial rewards of waged employment, whilst at the same time avoiding the 'constraints' they associate with it. Furthermore, they might use *trucs* (tricks) to get by, despite their low socio-economic status.

8. This expression is taken from Ruquoy and Hiernaux (1986).

9. As far as Belgium is concerned, the facts referred to are given by Ruquoy and Hiernaux (1986), and by Belgeonne (1984). Data referring to France, which looks rather similar, may be found in Gokalp (1981).

10. See particularly Galland (1985).

11. In Belgium, whilst 55 per cent of young foreign women are active between the ages of 20 and 25, only 30 per cent remain so after the age of 25.

References

Bastenier, A., Dassetto, F. and Fonck, H. (1986), *La Situation de Formation Professionnelle des Jeunes Étrangers en Belgique*, Centre Européen pour le développement de la formation professionnelle, Berlin: Document.

Belgeonne, N. (1984), 'Crise et transformation de la valeur travail chez les jeunes ouvriers', Louvain-la-Neuve: mémoire Université Catholique de Louvain (unpublished paper).

Bertaux, M. (1977), *Destins Personnels et Structure de Classe*, Paris: Presses Universitaires de France.

Bourdieu, P. (1974), 'Avenir de classe et causalité du probable', *Revue Française de Sociologie*, **XV**, 1, pp. 3–42.

Campioli, G. (1977), 'Enfants migrants et réussite scolaire: les exceptions', *Recherches Sociologiques*, **VIII**, 2, pp. 245–73.

Dassetto, F. and Bastenier, A. (1982), *La deuxième génération d'immigrés italiens en Belgique: Analyse du processus d'inserton sociale et professionnelle*, Working Papers United Nations Development Program/International Labour Organization. Geneva: BIT.

Dassetto, F. and Bastenier, A. (1984), *L'Islam Transplanté. Vie et Organisation des Minorités Musulmanes de Belgique*, Anvers: Editions EPO.

Galland, O. (1985), *Les Jeunes*, Paris: Editions La Découverte.

Glazer, N. and Moynihan, D. P. (eds) (1975), *Ethnicity: Theory and Experience*, Cambridge, Mass: Harvard University Press

Gokalp, C. (1981), *Quant Vient L'Âge des Choix. Enquête Auprès des Jeunes de 18 a 25 Ans: Emploi, Résidence, Mariage*, INED, Paris: Presses Universitaires de France

Gordon, Milton (1964), *Assimilation in American Life. The Role of Race, Religion and National Origins*, New York: Oxford University Press.

Kusznuski, J. (1967), *Les Origines de la Classe Ouvrière*, Paris: Hachette.

Lienard, G. and Servais, E. (1975), *Capital Culturel et Inégalités Sociales*, Brussels: Editions Vie Ouvrière

OECD (1975), *L'OCDE et les Migrations Internationales*, Paris: OECD.

OECD (1978), *La Chaîne Migratoire*, Paris: OECD.

Ruquoy, D. and Hiernaux, J. P. (1986), *Travail: Ras le Bol? Jouissance? Le Travail Vu par des Jeunes Travailleurs et Chômeurs*, Brussels: Editions Vie Ouvrière.

Author index

Subject index

Training Opportunities Scheme
(TOPS) 59
Youth Opportunity Programme
(YOP) 59, 60, 77, 80, 82
Youth Task Group Report 60, 61,
78
Youth Training Scheme (YTS)
59–62 *passim*, 77–80 *passim*,
82, 83

National Dwelling and Household
Survey 69
national origins of foreigns 6, 7, 92
National Programme of Research
into Occupational Training 35
Nationality Act (1947) 62
naturalization, difficulty of 25, 53
North Atlantic Treaty
Organization (NATO) 114

occupational training
Germany 127–9
Switzerland, access to 37–41
Occupational Training Bill 38
occupations, numbers in various
types 126
Office Fédéral de la Statistique
(OFS), Switzerland 27, 31, 37
Statistiques des élèves 34, 35, 37
Office of Population Censuses &
Surveys (OPCS) 62
Organization for Economic Co-
operation and Development
(OECD) 2, 11, 13, 14, 16, 21,
28, 52, 111, 116, 153
La chaine migratoire 172–3n
SOPEMI 6, 7

Policy Studies Institute (PSI) 85
Projektgruppe 134
proletariat
settled 151–2, 153, 154
and youths 151, 156
'protection' against foreigners 116

Race Relations Act (1976) 81
racism 91, 104
recession
reduction in migrant labour,
Switzerland 29–30

1974–6 and 1981–3 29
recruitment of foreign labour,
Germany 114, 115
refugees, south-east Asian in
France 90
residence permits, France 97
return orientation and work values
138–9

school
attainment 118–21 *passim*
attendance 118, 119; by
nationality 120
self-employment
France 96, 102–3
immigrants 30, 43–4
plans for 164, 165, 171
Senator für Schulwesen 123, 125
service sector jobs, growth 57, 125
settlement
and community formation 139–
40
without assimilation 141
without identification 141
social hierarchy, foreigners in
France 90
social stratum in lower social
milieu by nationality 46, 47
socialization of immigrants 19,
155–6, 157, 158
socially insured active population
146
'SOS Racism' movement 104
SPRESE 95
Statistiches Bundesamt 124, 127
status 115–16
lack of 126
stratification 9–10, 17, 18, 20
immigrant workers 46–7, 49
sub-proletariat 19, 20
potential formation 165, 172
Swiss Science Council 31
Switzerland, size of foreign
population 6, 24

training
post-compulsory, standards 40
United Kingdom emphasis on
59–62